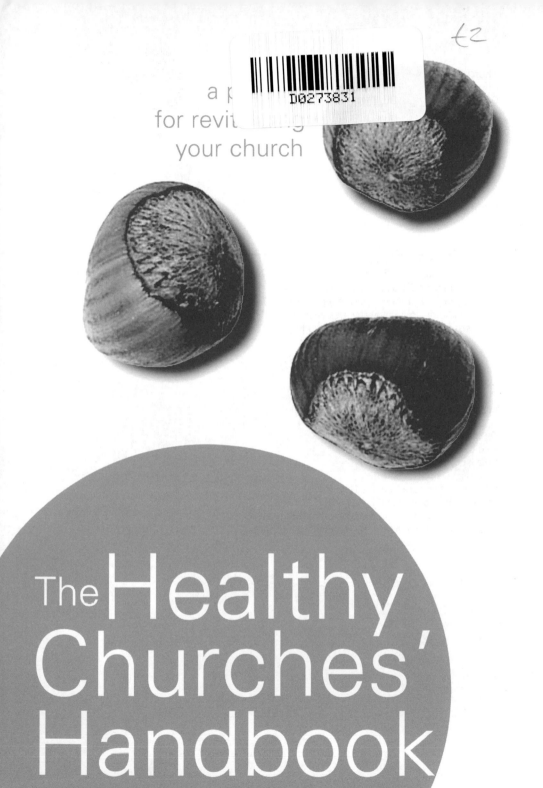

a practical guide
for revitalizing
your church

The Healthy Churches' Handbook

Robert Warren

CHURCH HOUSE
PUBLISHING

Church House Publishing
Church House
Great Smith Street
London SW1P 3NZ

ISBN 0 7151 4017 5

Published 2004 by Church House Publishing
Second impression 2004

Tel: 020 7898 1594
Fax: 020 7898 1449
Email: copyright@c-of-e.org.uk

Cover design by Church House Publishing

Printed in England by
The Cromwell Press Ltd,
Trowbridge, Wiltshire

Contents

Foreword

Many congregations around Britain have already benefited from
Growing Healthy Churches. It is good that this material has now been
conveniently gathered together for wider circulation in this handbook.
Here, churches are enabled 'to take a snapshot' of their life together,
measure it against seven well-proven marks of a healthy congregation,
and act on their conclusions. In some ways, it provides for parish
development what the *Emmaus* programme does for individual spiritual
growth. However, anyone seeking a quick fix for ailing churches will
be disappointed. These signposts on the journey towards a greater
corporate Christ-likeness will take time, honesty and commitment to
work through together.

Bishops often refer to this journey when instituting a new parish priest,
but it is not always clear how the hopes raised at such a time can be
realized in practice. Congregations are not always good in assessing their
strengths and weaknesses. Some churches all too easily focus on the
things they cannot do, and in their discouragement find it difficult to
recognize and celebrate what is good about their life together. In others,
able women and men possessing the highest motives can be broken by
an unwillingness to move on from entrenched attitudes having deep roots
in past history. Hence the importance given in this handbook to appointing
an external facilitator to help the process along.

The materials here are amazingly adaptable. They can be used with whole
congregations, leadership groups and with home groups, with churches
of any size and location, at any stage in the life of a parish. There are ideas
here for teaching, discussion and meditation. The unusual 'angel' material
turns good theology into an imaginative tool that will particularly help
those who think visually to make their full contribution towards the next
steps in fulfilling the vocation of their church. In the Rochester Diocese,
this programme has so far touched nearly two-thirds of the benefices. It
appeals to every style of church – and to Archdeacons as well! Our hope
and prayer is that it will bless your congregation as we have seen it bless
many others.

Carol Kitchener, Parish Development Officer
Michael Howard, Bishop's Officer for Mission
Diocese of Rochester

How the book works

This practical guide helps churches identify their strengths and weaknesses and discover what action to take in order to develop the health of their church. The focus is on the *quality* of the church's life rather than just the numbers attending.

Churches are helped to assess themselves against seven marks of a healthy church. The goal is not easy solutions, but rather encountering the reality of God's presence in and through the life of each church.

The seven marks of a healthy church are:

1. Energized by faith
2. Outward-looking focus
3. Seeks to find out what God wants
4. Faces the cost of change and growth
5. Operates as a community
6. Makes room for all
7. Does a few things and does them well

Part 1 – Exploring the marks of healthy churches

Chapter 1 – Discovering healthy churches		The story of how the 'model' of seven marks of a healthy church was developed
Chapter 2 – Living the two great commandments	Unpacking Marks 1 & 2	What it means to be energized by faith and to develop an outward looking focus
Chapter 3 – Costly calling	Unpacking Marks 3 & 4	What is involved in seeking to find out what God wants, and in facing the cost of change and growth
Chapter 4 – Sign of the kingdom	Unpacking Marks 5, 6 & 7	What it means to operate as a community, make room for all and do a few things well

Part 2 – Growing healthy churches

Chapter 5 – Embarking on the healthy journey	Doing the Church Profile Exercise
Chapter 6 – Developing healthy churches	Taking action
Chapter 7 – Facilitating healthy churches	Using a facilitator to aid the process

Part 3 – Seeing the whole picture

Chapter 8 – What is church?	Unpacking what we mean by church
Chapter 9 – The angel of the church	Developing a Church Profile from an intuitive and imaginative angle

Part 4 – Healthy churches exercises

Chapter 10 – Preparing for the Church Profile Exercise	Practical materials for doing
Chapter 11 – The Church Profile Exercise	• the Church Profile Exercise and
Chapter 12 – Angel of the Church Exercises	• the Angel of the Church Exercises

Downloading all handouts

Handouts for all the exercises may be photocopied from the Appendices. They may also be downloaded from the web: go to www.chpublishing.co.uk/healthychurches

Introduction

This book is for anyone who cares about the well-being of the Church.

In the changed and changing world in which we live that well-being can easily come under threat and shift from an experienced reality into what feels like an unattainable dream. The good news is that there are answers – not easy ones or neat ones – rather, ones that have to be hammered out on the anvil of the local church's experience. But churches, across the country and beyond, are finding that it is possible to plot the health of a church, identify actions to address areas of weakness and embark on a journey to greater wholeness.

That is what this book is about. It is designed as much for lay members of the church as it is clergy. Not least since it is often lay members of churches who first raise questions about the health of the church and prompt the use of material such as is contained in this book.

It is called a *Handbook* because it is not intended simply to be an outline of a theory but a practical guide to help churches identify where work needs to be done to enrich their health – then take action. So stories, exercises and explanation are all included in this book.

A journey of discovery

What is offered here represents the fruit of over ten years of research and reflection on how the Church can best express its faith and life in today's setting.

In the first of those years, whilst working at the Church of England's Board of Mission, based in Church House, Westminster, I wrote *Building Missionary Congregations*.[1] That fifty-five page booklet looked at why the Church needs to reshape its life in today's largely post-Christendom context. It traced an outline of what that reshaping might look like. Having written the booklet, I then found myself involved with a fascinating, diverse and stimulating number of people and churches who were seeking to express, in the reality of actual local church life, some of the things I had written about.

That involvement continued when, in 1998, I moved to work full-time with *Springboard*, a small team set up by the Archbishops of Canterbury and

York as an Initiative for Evangelism. During its life (1991–2003), that team has sought to help the Church find appropriate ways to communicate its faith, accompany the great number of people today who are on a journey to faith, and enable each church so to order its life that it becomes translucent of the gospel.

One person with whom I worked while in both these posts has been Dr Janet Hodgson, the Adviser in Local Mission in the Durham Diocese (1994–2002). It was she who invited me to meet with representatives from churches in that diocese that had experienced significant growth in the first half of the 1990s. It looked like, and proved to be, a most stimulating day. What neither of us had imagined was quite what would result from that. It was the start of a journey of discovery.

Part 1: Exploring the marks of a healthy church

That initial day in Durham, and the subsequent reflections on it, yielded a number of insights, not least that these churches shared common characteristics. They were subsequently developed as *the seven marks of a healthy church*. The story of how this came into being is told in Chapter 1, *Discovering healthy churches*. The following three chapters (Chapter 2, *Living the two great commandments*, Chapter 3, *Costly calling*, Chapter 4, *Sign of the kingdom*) explore these marks in detail. They contain descriptions and stories of how these marks work out in practice in a wide range of church settings, sizes and traditions. A summary page of all the marks follows at the end of Part 1.

An intriguing question in this whole process has been 'why *these* marks?' Why are *these* the characteristics of a healthy church? This is explored further in the text, but here it needs to be said that the marks are a good description of the values that Christ himself expressed in his life and which the disciple today is called upon to live out.

So these marks of a healthy church are not some management tool for running the church more efficiently and effectively (though they can doubtless have those positive effects), but are signposts on the journey of faith. The journey towards health for a church is along the path of expressing the life of Christ. Healthy churches are on pilgrimage.

Part 2: Growing healthy churches

It quickly became clear that, for all the churches involved, the present good state of health was the result of a long journey of discipleship and discovery. Indeed, a commitment to making that journey towards health was not only a distinguishing mark of these churches but also an important signpost for others seeking to strengthen the life of their church. Making a long-term commitment to develop the quality and vitality of a church is the key to health. The nature and implications of this commitment are explored in Chapter 5, *Embarking on the healthy journey.*

Setting out on that journey begins, like all journeys, with a single step. In this case the step is doing what is called the Church Profile Exercise. Done with a leadership group, such as a church council, or with a 'whole church group', this exercise introduces people to the seven marks of a healthy church. Participants are then asked to score their church on all these marks. The individual scores are transcribed onto a single, large (flipchart sized) sheet. This gives an immediate profile of the church. From it can be read off strengths and weaknesses and other indicators. Out of reflection on this it is usually possible to identify where action is needed.

Chapters 10 and 11 describe the Church Profile Exercise and give guidance about how to conduct it as part of the practical material in the last part of the book.

Managing both the Church Profile Exercise and the consequent process of identifying where action is needed and setting about taking that action and monitoring it are covered in Chapter 6, *Developing healthy churches.* Chapter 7 (*Facilitating healthy churches*) explores the value of drawing on external help in this whole process, together with an outline of the task of achieving these goals.

Part 3: Seeing the whole picture

Because of the way that the marks of a healthy church have been developed, they do not constrain churches into one mould, but rather open doors to new expressions and to surprising developments. They also provoke questions about the very nature of the Church.

One of the most fundamental questions raised in this work with churches is addressed in Chapter 8, *What is church?* The issues surrounding this question provoke us to see the Church as a whole organization or 'system', with its own discernible ethos, identity and spirit.

Having begun to address that more fundamental question of what church is, we stumbled across the strange subject of the angel of the church. This is a phrase taken from the letters of the risen Christ addressed to the churches in Revelation 2 and 3. Engaging with this concept opened up a whole new dimension to working with churches, for it comes at the subject from an intuitive and imaginative angle rather than from the analytical approach of working with the marks of a healthy church.

How we came across this approach and the use and value of this way of seeing church are explored in Chapter 9, *The angel of the church*.

Experience suggests that working with this concept of the angel of the church can help churches hear and respond to the call of God on their corporate life and thus reflect more of the divine wholeness and salvation that Christ came to bring.

Part 4: Healthy churches exercises

The last section of the book is devoted to practical materials churches can work with. First comes material about the Church Profile Exercise. Chapter 10 (*Preparing for the Church Profile Exercise*) is designed to equip anyone seeking to carry out the exercise. The programme for that exercise is set out in Chapter 11 (*The Church Profile Exercise*). Chapter 12 (*Angel of the Church Exercises*) gives a number of suggestions about how churches can explore the subject of the angel of the church and use that material to gain insights about their church and the call of Christ to it today. Finally, the *Resources for healthy churches* section gives a list of courses, books, websites and other resources that can help in working on each of the marks of a healthy church.

To those who are familiar with *Growing Healthy Churches*

The initial research was published by *Springboard* in a booklet entitled *Growing Healthy Churches*. That booklet was distributed to all clergy as part of the *Restoring Hope in our Church* resource, in 2003. To those familiar with that booklet and those who have already done a Church Profile Exercise (previously called the *Church Checklist*) it is worth pointing out what new material is contained in this Handbook. It contains a good deal of material and insights gained since the publication of *Growing Healthy Churches* as well as much that could not be included in a twelve-page booklet. Additionally available in this book are:

■   A much enlarged and updated exploration of the marks of a healthy church, together with stories of how they are being expressed in a great variety of churches. This material is set out in Part 1.

■   Materials needed to conduct the Church Profile Exercise and to help churches identify where action is needed. It is also designed to help plan and take action to enrich its health. The aim here is to make this Handbook an accessible resource for developing the life and health of a church. This material is set out in Part 2.

- Resources and guidance for addressing the underlying questions that are often raised about what we mean by 'church'. It also includes an introduction to the subject of the angel of a church with help as to how to use this approach. This is contained in Part 3.

- Matters concerning the use of an external facilitator, including guidance about how to be one, are addressed in Chapter 7, *Facilitating healthy churches.*

- A guide to a wide range of resources likely to help churches develop any of the marks.

The practical nature of the exercises is what make this a *Handbook* for churches wanting to develop their health and give expression to the life of Christ in and through the life of the church. It contains the material to *do* what the book is talking about.

Natural Church Development

Not long after the material on which this book is based had been developed and was being used around the country, *Natural Church Development,*[2] by Christian Schwarz was published in England. It resonates with much contained in this book, not least in its emphasis on the nurturing of the qualitative side of church life, rather than majoring on numerical growth. It has helped in the development of *Growing Healthy Churches* at a number of points, which are referred to in the text.

However, there are differences. They are not primarily about where the approach of this book conflicts with *Natural Church Development*, but rather about approaches that, though different, are complementary. Among those differences are the following points:

- The key difference, explained more fully in the text, is that the marks of a healthy church identified here are expressed in terms of values, goals and characteristics (e.g. 'operates as a community') whereas in *Natural Church Development* they are expressed in terms of activities ('holistic small groups').

- The *Healthy Churches* material is a lighter structure, enabling a church to take a 'health check' in one three-hour session.

- *Healthy Churches* has a much lower 'doctrine of numbers' and sees any statistics as a helpful guide rather than in any sense an accurate measure of where a church is at. For example, *Natural Church Development* can talk in terms of the leadership of a church being rated as '64.6%'. The *Healthy Churches* material does not provide any such quantifiable measure; though it does help churches identify strengths, weaknesses and issues needing to be addressed.

Tested material

This material has, in one way or another, been extensively used across the Church of England in the last seven years. Several dioceses, in a range of different ways, have taken up the material and used it.

Durham Diocese was where it all began. Although it was never used in any systematic way across the diocese, it was used by the Mission Enablers to help churches reflect on their life together and by archdeacons, who used it as a basis for parts of their annual visitation returns.

Coventry Diocese was the first to make use of it as a whole diocesan process. Their involvement was of great value in the way that they were willing to try out, and to adapt, the material offered. It continues to be the basis for much of the resourcing of the churches in the diocese.

That was followed by *Rochester* Diocese, whose use of the material is the most long term and extensive to date. It has become the central framework of reference for its mission and parish development work. Their involvement has greatly contributed to the development of the work, not least in the use of facilitators.

Next came the *Carlisle* Diocese, where the material has been used quite differently. Every church was asked to do the Church Profile Exercise as part of a programme in which every parish was to be visited by a member of the bishop's staff team. Those staff team members then went to churches and listened to their answers to the questions 'what did you learn from doing this exercise?', 'what action are you now planning to take?' and 'how can the diocese help you with that?' A diocesan strategy document is now being developed out of that extensive process of listening to churches.

The *York* Diocese has used the material on an area and deanery basis rather than as a whole diocese. It has proved another fruitful area of learning for all concerned, particularly as the focus there has been on small, sometimes isolated, rural churches.

Chichester Diocese has more recently started working with the material and developed an extensive and long-term programme for its use in the diocese. The process, ably led by the Diocesan Missioner, the Revd John Twisleton, involves training and deployment of facilitators. The material is also being used in the diocese as a way of helping churches during a vacancy to think about the life of the church and so identify the sort of leadership they need for the next phase of the church's life.

The recently appointed Canon Missioner of *Bradford* Diocese, the Revd David Brierley, has developed a process of working with churches using the *Healthy Churches* material as the framework. Inevitably, where there is just one person working, the rate of coverage of the diocese is slower, yet it has the advantage of being rooted long term in the whole process of nurturing the life of churches.

Similarly, the Revd John Gooding, Parish Development Officer in the *Guildford* Diocese, has been using this material as the primary tool for his engagement with churches and has tested the material extensively and added to the insights of this book.

In a number of dioceses it is used to help churches during a vacancy to reflect on their life together and the needed future direction. This forms the backdrop to considering what sort of new leader is needed. In other dioceses, new incumbents are encouraged to use it a year or two into the ministry as a way of taking stock and mapping future direction once they have become familiar with the situation.

Apart from all these group and area uses, this material has been used by an unknown number of individual churches across the country.

Although this material emerged from the Church of England, it has also been used in several other denominations. *The Healthy Churches' Handbook* is not restricted in its relevance to the Church of England. It has certainly proved of value and is fully accessible to Baptist, Methodist and URC churches. It has also been used in chaplaincy situations in Europe and in several dioceses in Australia.

An accompanied journey

Though the itinerant ministry is often a lonely one, this has been anything but a journey on my own. So many have been a support, stimulus and challenge on the way, as well as those from whom I have learned much during these years.

Dr Janet Hodgson has been especially crucial in keeping me on the straight and narrow. Or is it getting me off it? It was she who got us both into the *Healthy Churches* material, quite unintentionally, as the reader will discover. She has been with me on the whole journey, working on the initial marks, writing it up in the *Springboard* Resource Paper, *Growing Healthy Churches*, presenting the material, particularly in the Coventry and (early part of the engagement with) the Rochester Dioceses. Since she retired to her homeland of South Africa we have continued to correspond and she has been a marvellous 'critical friend', reliving her academic past by marking my frequent texts. In a very real sense this material is ours rather than just mine, though I accept full responsibility for what follows.

More recently, the Revd Alison White (who happened to be Janet's predecessor as Adviser in Local Mission in the Durham Diocese) has shared with me in presenting, shaping and refining, the material now being offered to the wider Church. Alison has been a wonderful colleague, able to pick up and run with material that was already well formed. Part of what I think I have to offer, because of my particular temperament and personality, is seeing patterns that can give churches 'a track to run on'. Alison's gift, and mission, has been to deconstruct all patterns and structures and to open up me, and the material, to as much messiness as she could smuggle in! It has helped in large measure, I hope, to avoid what follows being over-tidy, restrictive, or too narrowly programmatic. There is certainly no desire or intention to try to conform every church to a single expression. My sincere hope is that *The Healthy Churches' Handbook* will open up, rather than close down, options and possibilities.

The Revd Canon Mavis Wilson, now Rector of Frimley, but previously one of the longest serving Diocesan Missioners (in her case, in the Guildford Diocese) has also been of enormous help to me in developing this material. She has been 'facilitator-in-chief' and run a number of training sessions for those involved in various ways in helping churches to do the Church Profile Exercise and to develop plans to enrich the health of the church. I came as a novice to the work of facilitation and owe Mavis an enormous amount for teaching me at least the rudiments of that discipline. How much easier it is to tell others what to think and do rather than help them work that out for themselves!

There are so many others who have helped on the way. The Revd Paul Simmonds did sterling work in enabling the material to be used for the first time in a whole diocese (Coventry). He would not let us rest until engaging with children and young people was firmly part of the material.

The Revd Canon Michael Howard and the Revd Carol Kitchener from the Rochester Diocese have been brilliant at taking our material and integrating it into the mission agenda, and beyond, of the whole diocese. They also edited a fine series of home studies on the material for the *Church of England Newspaper* during Lent 2003. Alison and I, who have worked with them the most, have been so impressed, and instructed, by the way they have taken, developed, and 'translated' the material and then done a masterly job of finding, training, deploying and supporting facilitators of healthy churches. They really have grasped the long-term nature of this process and helped to draw something like 70 per cent of the churches in the diocese to engage in some measure with the material.

The Revd John Gooding, Parish Development Officer in the Guildford Diocese, has probably done more work with local churches using both *Building Missionary Congregations* and *Growing Healthy Churches*, than anyone else in the country (certainly more than me). I have greatly valued his quiet, perceptive and practical observations, as well as his consistent encouragement to press on.

Both Bishop Colin Bennetts of Coventry and Bishop Graham Dow of Carlisle have, by inviting me and others to work with the whole of their respective dioceses, enabled us to test the material with hundreds of churches in quite different settings. It has resulted in learning much and gaining insight from many, with whom it has been a privilege to work.

At the heart of this whole project has been the conviction and prayer that the Church of Jesus Christ might be just that: a church that gives expression to the life of Christ in all that it is and does. This is the prayer and vision that have sustained and undergirded all that has been done. This book is offered with the same prayerful desire of the apostle Paul when he expressed his vision for the Church as leading to the time when:

> ... all of us come to the unity of the faith and of the knowledge of the Son of God, to maturity, to the measure of the full stature of Christ.[3]

May God in his goodness use this book to assist in that holy journey of the Church which, by his Spirit, he has brought into being.

Part 1:
Exploring the marks
of healthy churches

Chapter 1
Discovering healthy churches

The processes outlined in this book for strengthening the vitality of a church did not happen by design or as the result of some splendid theory. They have grown out of what was planned as a single day event in one diocese. The story of that day and what resulted from it is worth recounting.

In 1996, the observant Adviser in Local Mission, Dr Janet Hodgson, had been looking through the attendance figures for the diocese from 1990 to 1995. She noted two highly contrasting figures. Overall, the Sunday attendance figures for the diocese showed a 16 per cent decline in these five years, hardly a sign of health in the first half of the Decade of Evangelism.

Yet more striking was another figure. Of the 260 churches in the diocese, 25 *had grown by over 16 per cent during the same period.* So these churches had 'bucked the trend' by a remarkable 32 per cent divergence from the overall picture. A further group of churches had grown by between 1 per cent and 15 per cent, but it was decided to focus on those that had mirrored the overall decline by their growth. This was both because 25 churches were quite enough to be working with and also because 16 per cent was a big enough figure to ensure that we were not dealing with statistical error rather than church growth.

Not surprisingly, Dr Janet Hodgson started to ask 'why'? Some of the more common explanations just did not fit. Were they all the larger churches? Were they all charismatic/evangelical 'church growth enthusiasts'? Were they all the comfortable middle-class churches in the leafy suburbs? Were they Urban Priority Area (UPA) parishes generously funded by the Church Urban Fund? Were they all churches led by the youngest, most visionary, enthusiastic and able clergy? The answer was 'no' in every case.

The most obvious thing about these churches was their sheer variety. Between them they represented 15 of the 16 deaneries in the diocese. They represented all social settings: urban, suburban, inner city, rural, ex-mining communities. Every social setting in the diocese was represented by at least one of these churches. A full range of church traditions was represented with no one tradition having an unusually large contingent. All church sizes were equally represented.

These churches were being led by a good cross section of clergy. The whole age spread was represented by the clergy present. As far as could be judged, a wide range of personality types and leadership styles was represented too. There were enthusiasts and more reflective types. Some were very clear and confident of their faith whilst others were of a quieter and more questioning disposition.

Even before the day took place, this striking range of types and settings of churches and their leadership was seen as seriously good news. No context, no size of church, no church tradition, no leadership style seemed closed to the possibility of significant growth. So what was the secret of their varied stories? It was hoped that a day spent with them would begin to unlock some answers to that intriguing question.

Making sense of what was heard

One hundred people from these 25 churches came to the day. It was a most stimulating and energizing experience for all concerned, which left a mass of anecdotes, impressions, facts and feelings to assimilate.

One of the first things that stood out was that none of the churches seemed to have been majoring on being *growing* churches. Numbers were not a big issue for them. Much more typical was the sense that these churches were seeking to 'be the church better'. What they were doing was taking their faith seriously and seeking to be church to the very best of their ability. So describing them as growing churches did not capture the essence of their story. Their attention was on quality rather than quantity. This is why *healthy* seemed a truer description of what was going on than *growing*. Indeed, some had to be persuaded that they were growing and should come to the day. So none of them were making growth in numbers attending church a major part of their strategy. The growth had much more to do with the principle of nature that growth is one of the more obvious signs of a healthy organism.

The churches in this initial day had been invited simply because their numbers had increased. The reason for that was that it is the most accessible way to identify good things going on in a church. In fact, they had identified themselves simply as a result of someone looking at the diocesan attendance figures. Finding out how far a church is healthy is a much more difficult and complex matter. Indeed, this whole book is devoted to that process.

Defining terms

The words 'growing' and 'healthy' have already been used in relation to churches, so it is good to define what is meant by those terms.

The normal understanding of the words 'grow' and 'growth' in connection with the life of the church is in terms of numerical growth. However, in the phrase *growing healthy churches*, 'growing' describes our task of nurturing the life of the church as in growing a healthy rose bush.

When it comes to the use of the words 'health' and 'healthy', we must recognize that we live in a culture that has an unhealthy attitude to health. Our culture sees health as a right that should be ours. It is thought of in terms of freedom from pain and – often – freedom from the ageing process. So to be healthy is thought to be synonymous with being fit, good looking, young and fully in control of our mental faculties. But is that a healthy view of health?

The particular way in which health is understood throughout this book is as a translation of the biblical concept of salvation, namely wholeness, balance and harmony with God and all creation. Christ frequently said to people whom he healed, 'your faith has saved you'. This is variously translated 'made you well', 'made you whole'. So a healthy church is one that has been touched and energized by the presence of God so it reflects something of the good news of the wholeness made possible through the knowledge of God as revealed in Christ, by the Holy Spirit.

Marks or activities?

When it came to expressing the insights gained from the churches involved in this day it was clear that a choice had to be made. In *Natural Church Development*[1] the approach is to describe roles and activities such as *empowering leadership* and *inspiring worship services*.

It was decided not to follow this approach, for two reasons. First, it did not do justice to what we were seeing, which was more about an attitude or a value rather than primarily about particular activities. Second, it was judged important, because of the sheer diversity of the ways that these churches expressed their life, not to suggest that particular activities were necessarily the key.

One of the clearest illustrations of this point concerned small groups. Most of the churches whose story we heard did have small groups that played an important part in their growth. But not all had such groups. In any case, there was something more important underlying those groups. These churches operated as a community with an openness in personal relationships that took the church well beyond operating simply as organization. Our observation was that these churches were loving communities that usually found small groups a helpful way of giving expression to that. The goal, however, was to be a loving community.

Small groups were simply one of the most usual ways of giving expression to that goal.

All of this resulted in the marks of a healthy church being formulated in terms of goals, characteristics, values and aspirations, rather than activities.

This is also valuable in view of the emerging new ways of being church. It was thought important not to constrain churches into any particular organizational shape. So, for example, some new ways of expressing the life of a church may have worship built into how they operate rather than as an activity as such. Thinking in terms of values and goals means that a growing variety of expressions of church life can all connect with these marks.

Establishing common characteristics

The initial Durham day had been conceived as a one-off. Having done it, and seen so many striking overlaps in the emphasis of widely different churches, it became clear that a list of common themes would be worth producing. Over the years they have evolved a little and been sharpened up but are essentially the same as originally seen. That evolution is due to a similar exercise having been repeated in four other dioceses.

Those repeated themes, now called 'marks', can be summarized as follows.

Energized by faith seems to be a foundational characteristic. At the heart of these churches and their members is a reality about their awareness of the presence, goodness and love of God. Faith is the fuel on which these churches run.

Outward-looking focus. These churches were typified not by concentrating on their own life and concerns but by a practical care for the local context, the whole of life and the world in which we live. They are marked by a capacity to enjoy life and feel the pain of the struggles in our world.

Seeks to find out what God wants. There is a sharpness of focus and seriousness of purpose about such churches, which are carried forward by a sense of divine vocation rather than stuck in a dull repetition of past assumptions and patterns. Prayerfully they are on the move.

Faces the cost of change and growth. Individuals and groups are regularly faced with hard choices and testing circumstances. These churches evidenced the courage to face hard and painful truths and to be prepared to make real changes that were often costly.

Operates as a community. It is not just faith in God that sustains these churches but the reality and strength of generous and honest relationships that makes church 'family' for all who participate and draws out each person's gifts and contribution.

Makes room for all. Though they greatly value what they have, not least in their support of one another, these churches have found ways of making others not just welcome at services but part of the life of the church. Generosity permeates the life of these churches.

Does a few things and does them well. One of the most surprising characteristics of these churches, which results from a sense of responding to God's call on their time and effort, is the quiet purposefulness of their life. They are not rushing around madly but enjoying what they do and seeing the positive results of doing a quality job.

The journey on

Once having established the marks it was then possible to develop ways for other churches to use them to reflect on their own church life. A grid was produced that enabled each person to 'score' their church and so develop a corporate profile.

How this can be used is explained later, but first it is necessary to explore these marks in greater detail. That now follows in the next three chapters.

Chapter 2
Living the two great commandments

Energized by faith *and* an outward-looking focus

As vicar of a growing church I was sometimes asked about the causes of that growth by visitors to the church. It was usually put in the form of a question such as 'to what do you attribute the success of this church?' I recall not only feeling uncomfortable with the use of the word 'success', but stumped for an answer. Whenever I did mention something I was always aware of other factors too. With hindsight, and the help of the healthy churches work, I am much better placed to give an answer.

My struggle in the past was that the question assumed there was *one* thing that was the cause of such growth. This material indicates that there are *a number of factors* at work in such situations. Moreover, it is the interplay between those factors that is important.

Growing a healthy church is rather like baking a delicious cake. Good ingredients are a vital start. Then comes getting the proportions and mix right and knowing how long and at what temperature to cook it for. So with healthy churches, as indeed with healthy relationships, it is the interplay of a number of factors that enables things to work well. This guide through the marks will also include pointers as to where and how they interact with each other.

The exploration of these marks has a double purpose. First, it is designed to help church leaders and members understand the things that matter most in a church. Second, it is given so that anyone presenting the marks in a church context has material to draw on for such a task.

This chapter covers the first two marks, being *energized by faith* and having *an outward-looking focus*. These first marks focused on a church's fundamental relationships: with God and with the world around it. As churches work to develop their relationship to God and to their context, both they and the individuals who make up the church will be making a journey further into living out the two great commandments – to love God and others.

First mark: energized by faith

Mark 1: energized by faith
rather than just keeping things going or trying to survive

- *worship and sacramental life*: move people to experience God's love
- *motivation*: energy comes from a desire to serve God and one another
- *engages with Scripture*: in creative ways that connect with life
- *nurtures faith in Christ*: helping people to grow in, and share, their faith.

Whilst all the marks are important this one rightly stands at the head of the list and is the entry point into health for any church, since from it all the other marks flow.

Some churches lack any internal energy. Everything is an enormous effort. As one person put it: 'our church is like a wheelbarrow, nothing moves unless you push it'.

Other churches have energy, but not necessarily from an entirely healthy source. Energy may come from a desire to keeping a medieval building in good condition, from having the best set of bell-ringers for miles, or from wanting to boast the finest choral tradition in the town. Energy can also come from making sure 'our group' keeps control. Equally, energy may come simply from a desire to keep things as they are, or just keeping things going. Survival is a powerful motivator. Most of these things are not wrong in themselves but they are not sufficient as the foundational basis for the life of a church, which is a community of disciples of Jesus Christ.

> The bishop in one diocese recounted how he had to go to one church and tell them that it was no longer viable to keep their church open. It would be closing in a year's time. Only, it did not. The prospect of closure so energized the members that they started to share their faith and work in a number of ways for the well-being of the church. A year later it was doing so well that the bishop withdrew the threat. But he was emboldened to go and say the same thing to another church the next year. History repeated itself and that church began to flourish too. The same happened in the third year.
>
> It would be interesting to discover how such churches stand in relation to the marks of a healthy church outlined in this book. All three churches had discovered new energy. This

> may have lead to a deeper connection (even re-connection) with the faith. It might, however, have all been the fruit of the church's being energized by closure. There is nothing necessarily wrong with that, but, if that does not lead on to being energized by faith, there will be something seriously lacking in the life and well-being of such churches.

It is faith in God as revealed in Jesus Christ by the Holy Spirit that is the source of vitality in the life of a healthy church. Different traditions express this in a variety of ways but, in all of them, prayer is a natural part of personal and church life, faith is talked about as a natural part of life and conversation, and the name of Christ is not a source of embarrassment.

Some of the particular ways in which this mark has been observed in churches are as follows:

■ *worship and sacramental life*: **move people to experience God's love**

There is a subtle yet profound difference between 'taking the service' and 'leading worship'. The focus of the former is on following the liturgy or order of service. The focus of the latter is on helping people to encounter the presence of God. This is likely to involve an ability to be comfortable with the use of *silence* to enable people to hear what God is saying to them. Equally, the use of *testimonies and stories*, in which people share experiences of God's action, are likely to be evident. A sense of *celebration* of the reality and goodness of God will be present. This is likely to be balanced by an ability, corporately, to engage with the pain and brokenness in the world around. So joy and sorrow, laughter and tears, will be in evidence.

> A rural church has seen significant growth, not because more people are coming to the services on Sunday but because several home communions, initially for house-bound individuals, have grown – 'by word of mouth'. The way that worship was being led was evidently connecting people with God and building a sense of belonging among those who come. This was becoming 'church' for them.

■ *motivation*: **energy comes from a desire to serve God and one another**

People want to serve God and one another, and this results in a sense of eagerness and enthusiasm around the place. Where this is *not* present, churches are likely to suffer from a *lack of energy*, with a very small group doing all the work. This sometimes happens because newcomers are kept out of active involvement in the life of the church for fear they might cause things to change.

Where there is motivation only from secondary matters it will often be seen in competing personal agendas, personality clashes and power struggles.

■ *engages with Scripture*: **in creative ways that connect with life**

This is more than simply claiming to be a church that 'preaches the Word' or whatever phrase resonates with any particular church tradition. Rather, it is about how Scripture is handled both in the pulpit and in personal and group reflection. Such churches are not afraid to wrestle with how the text of Scripture relates to life today and how it can and should be allowed to affect our values, choices and lifestyle.

> **One church did a Lent Bible study course on the theme of Jubilee. Out of this came a long-term engagement by the whole church with the campaign for Third World debt relief.**

> **Another church explored the issue of stress from a biblical perspective and came up with some 'stress-buster exercises' (meditations), which are now used by many in that church.**

■ *nurtures faith in Christ*: **helping people to grow in, and share, their faith**

In such churches faith is not assumed, but spoken about and seen as central to the task of the church. People are helped to reflect on their own experience of the grace and reality of God in their life – or to address the lack of it. They will be helped to tell their own story, whether of their earlier journey *to* faith or of their current experience of the journey *of* faith.

> **Prayer will play an important part in the life of such churches, both personal and corporate. Going on retreat, visiting a place of pilgrimage, having a spiritual director, or sharing in some prayer group or shared prayer discipline will be part of people's experience. Such churches are likely to be ones where Gerard Hughes' comment is being practised, namely that 'training in prayer should be the main preoccupation and service given by bishops and clergy to the adult members of the church'.[1]**

This frequently results in an awareness of sharing in a common enterprise that, at its heart, has a spiritual base. This will be so largely irrespective of whether a church Mission Statement exists or not.

In such churches, evangelism will be taking place irrespective of whether such sharing of the faith is organized or not – and largely irrespective of whether the word evangelism is used or not.

> A town-centre church produced a duplicated booklet of a dozen or so pages. Each page was written by one member of the church, telling the story of how their faith is nourished. It included a wide range of ways in which people are meeting God. At the end of each page a contact name or telephone number was given so that any regular member, or anyone coming new into the church, could follow up that particular track. By this means faith was being both expressed and nurtured.

Second mark: outward-looking focus

Mark 2: outward-looking focus
with a 'whole life' rather than a 'church life' concern

- deeply rooted in the *local community*, working in partnership with other denominations, faiths, secular groups and networks
- passionate and prophetic about *justice and peace*, locally and globally
- makes connections between *faith and daily living*
- responds to human need by *loving service*.

One of the striking characteristics of churches whose stories have been listened to in the healthy churches project has been the extent to which they have looked out beyond themselves and engaged with the whole of life and with the wider community. They are not ghetto churches, hiding from life. Rather, church is not the be-all and end-all of their existence. It is God's love for all creation and for all that is that motivates them – in the whole of their living.

These are churches that embody the truth that *we must stop starting with the church*. The starting point for these churches is the world around and the whole of life. They demonstrate in their life the truth that *no group is happy or healthy unless it has a task to fulfil beyond itself.*

- **deeply rooted *in the local community*, working in partnership with other denominations, faiths, secular groups and networks**

Churches of this sort do not need to know all the answers or always be the ones who solve problems. They are able to offer what they can and are willing to work as partners alongside others. In fact, they have a considerable knowledge of the local area, being aware of both the joys and sorrows around them, but are not inclined to push their solutions all the time.

> One such church, set in an ex-mining community, was sufficiently aware of what was happening that they described the community as in a state of 'frozen anger' about the closure of the pit at the time of the great Miners' Strike in the 1980s. Ten years on, when this anger seemed as real as the day the pit closed, the church realized that one of the reasons for this was that there had never been a 'funeral' for the pit. So the church held a service to mark the tenth anniversary of the closure. At it they gave thanks for the good times in the past and for all that the pit had meant to them. But they also had the courage to let some of the young people express their relief and delight that they would not have to spend their lives down a coal mine. This service resulted in a quite noticeable reduction in that sense of 'frozen anger' in the community. It also established better relationships between the church and that community.

■ **passionate and prophetic about *justice and peace*, locally and globally**

Such churches are living out the words of David Bosch that 'to participate in mission is to participate in love, for God is a fountain of sending love'.[2] They care about the world around them and their immediate locality too.

> The history of the Christian Church is full of the stories of people who did just this, including, in our own time, Mother Teresa of Calcutta's care for the poor, Martin Luther King's championing the cause of racial justice, Archbishop Desmund Tutu's call for the Church to be 'the rainbow people of God' joyfully celebrating racial diversity as a gift from God, and Dame Cicely Saunders' pioneering work in starting the hospice movement for care of the dying. Today, often in hidden and smaller ways, this passion is what many understand the Christian faith to be all about.
>
> At the local level, many churches have set up drop-in centres for the lonely, credit unions to help people cope with debt, small employment ventures to help the unemployed, language classes for new immigrants, and many other

such ventures that express God's generous care for all, not least the disadvantaged.

■ makes connections between *faith and daily living*

Too easily a person's 'ministry' is defined in terms of what they do in the life of the church. But the fact is that 'for the vast majority of laity . . . the main focus of their ministry lies in the opportunities presented by their everyday responsibilities'.[3] Healthy churches recognize that and work to equip church members to *live the faith* in the whole of life. They see this as of greater importance than getting everyone to do something in church. Indeed, this is the key to healthy evangelism, when people find in their faith the resources for living that help them make sense of life, live by a different set of values and have something to share with others about making sense of life.

> One church sought to do this by addressing the issue of low self-worth that they discerned was not only endemic in the local community but in the life of the church too. They adapted the Alcoholics Anonymous Twelve Step[4] programme, designing it for 'low-self-esteem-aholics'. They tested it and ran it first in the church and then made it available to the whole community.
>
> Another church, in a very different setting, found that their short course on Executive Stress was regularly attracting people with no previous connection with the church.

■ responds to human need by *loving service*

These churches are on the 'give' rather than the 'get'. They are operating on the abundance mentality of the gospel well expressed in the Christian Aid aim that 'all shall be included in the feast of life'.

This response is very striking, as in the care some churches show towards Asylum Seekers, and those who are disabled (or, as some prefer, 'differently abled') and Travellers. In other situations it is not so much a case of 'what you do', but 'how you do it', as illustrated in the following story.

> A church Parent-and-Toddler group became aware that they were operating in a subtle 'in-group' way that failed to express the generosity and welcome they had experienced through faith in Christ. In a typical session, the church members who led the group met in the kitchen for a good old gossip and left the isolated and lonely parents to cope

with their children and fend for themselves. Recognizing that this was 'unhealthy' ('unholy'), they decided to change things around. They kept two leaders in the kitchen but the other four went and sat with the parents and children. More than that, they sent four of the parents into the kitchen so they could join in some grown-up conversation. This leadership group was 'giving away' what they most valued. It led on to much closer relationships with the members of the group. Out of those relationships a number were given very practical help with major problems at home. Some found their way to faith in Christ through those friendships.

These are just some of the ways, and stories, of churches that have an attractive *outward-looking focus*. Such churches are full of stories of how God has been experienced 'out there' in daily life and in the local community. These are stories about things happening in the community, not just in the church. In such situations people sometimes cannot refrain from telling good news: 'we cannot keep from speaking about what we have seen and heard'.[5]

This healthy focus is often evident in the intercessions in Sunday services. They have an inclusive, life-affirming breadth that speaks of a good and generous God being worshipped in this place.

Churches with these characteristics are deeply attractive because their focus in not on themselves and their programmes but on God's goodness and reality and on the world around them. They are, indeed, living the two great commandments.

Chapter 3
Costly calling

Seeks to find out what God wants *and* faces the cost of change and growth

It was a brave and dangerous thing to become a follower of Christ in the Early Church as it still is across large parts of the world today. Ostracism, rejection by family and friends, loss of livelihood and even life, have all been the price that some of our fellow Christians have experienced.

To them, baptism made sense of the whole of life. They knew that being baptized into Christ's death and resurrection meant allowing that pattern to shape their lives. The Lord's Prayer was seen by many as a pattern of this, beginning, as it does, with dedication to the things of God (his name, kingdom and will) and then entrusting our needs to God's gracious provision.

This is the 'upside down' world of the kingdom of God that reverses the natural instinct to look after number one and only really to give if it does not inconvenience or affect us significantly.

Fascinatingly, healthy churches seem to have reconnected with this understanding of discipleship, not least at the corporate level. Church is 'practised' as a courageous following after Christ and a corporate willingness to engage in 'conversion' (the Greek word *metanoia* means both change of heart and change of mind) as a way of life. It is this costly seeking after and doing the will of God that is evident in the next two marks of a healthy church.

Third mark: seeks to find out what God wants

Mark 3: seeks to find out what God wants
discerning the Spirit's leading rather than trying to please everyone

- *vocation*: seeks to explore what God wants it to be and do
- *vision*: develops and communicates a shared sense of where it is going
- *mission priorities*: consciously sets both immediate and long-term goals
- able to call for, and make, *sacrifices*, personal and corporate, in bringing about the above and living out the faith.

It has been fascinating, over the years, to see how churches have stumbled over this mark. There is something deliberately awkward and unsettling about it. At one stage we used the term *clear sense of direction*. In the Western world we feel much more at home with that sort of language. It is about how we are sorting the church out and getting it properly organized. Once we get into that mindset we all too easily lapse into letting our own preferences set the church agenda. This is why we reverted to the more disturbing wording, which had been how we had first expressed this mark.

In much of the church there is a genuine desire to 'do something for God'. What these churches we had listened to had evidently found was a way of discovering what God wanted to do with them. It is God who sets the agenda of a healthy church – sometimes disturbingly so.

This mark starkly makes clear that the Church is first and foremost God's Church. Christ alone has died for his Church. It belongs to him. It is 'his Church' long before it was ever 'my church' or 'our church'. A healthy church acknowledges this by seeking to discover what God wants for and of *his* Church.

A tempting modification of this mark was to shorten it to *finds out what God wants*, but this did not do justice to what we observed. Some churches are so confident they know what God wants that they have long ago abandoned honest or earnest seeking after God's will. Such a 'know-all' attitude is a sign of disease, not health, in a church. There is a world of difference between Christ's promise that the truth would set us free[1] and an attitude that indicates that the truth has made us right.

A sense of struggle, questioning and the provisionality about how we understand what God wants of us is a mark of maturity for an individual and for a church. Health is found at least as much in the *seeking* as in the *finding*.

Some of the ways in which this mark is evident are as follows:

■   *vocation*: **seeks to explore what God wants it to be and do**

Both words are important here, being and doing. Indeed, our observation has been that healthy churches are more aware of, and put more effort into, their *being* than unhealthy churches. Healthy churches care about the quality of what is done, about how people feel, about the nature of the relationships within the church and the impact of the whole life of the church on a local community.

This sense of vocation is found in the lives of individual members who, being energized by faith, have a sense of God calling them to contribute what they do in and through the life of the church. This makes them less frantic, for they are simply following a sense of call rather than running around trying to do everything. Many churches needing someone to take on a task rely on giving out general notices, getting more desperate as time goes by, ending up pressurizing people to take on tasks for which they may be neither suited nor called.

> One church paid close attention to the way it filled posts in the life of the church. Those involved in the leadership of the particular piece of work, or those in overall leadership, first prayed about the task needing to be done and who might do it. They then went to individuals personally, inviting them to consider taking on the task. That invitation was always qualified by something like 'but we ask you to pray first before you give an answer'. Indeed, when it was the minister doing the inviting, he always added the further qualification 'if you do not discern that God is calling you to this you not only have my permission to say "no", you have a responsibility to God to say "no" to the minister'. There were often awkward gaps in the life of that church, but where things were being done they were done with creativity, excellence and great dedication, because people were motivated by a sense of divine call to them to do this piece of service.

But vocation has a corporate dimension as well. A whole church can sense that it is called of God to focus on a particular task at present. Where churches are seeking to discover God's will rather than get their own way, there is usually plenty of prayer, personal and corporate, conversation and consultation about the church's direction. An unhurried approach is the typical approach.

> The church council in one church decided that the buildings needed a major sort out. They appointed an architect, created a clear specification and had plans drawn up. They then took several months to share those plans with the church and to come together on several occasions to pray about whether this was what God wanted. Eventually the church council recognized that the church members were encouraging them to be more radical, and a more significant and substantial plan emerged. Those plans cost more, but people engaged in remarkably sacrificial giving. This was no doubt because they had been consulted and there was a

widespread sense of both ownership and awareness that 'God is calling us to this'.

This is in such contrast to many churches whose agendas and programmes are shaped by a variety of forces. These may include *external pressures* from the local community or wider church authorities who are wanting every church to 'do something about' a particular issue. Understandable though that pressure may be, it needs to be resisted in favour of the courage to seek to discover what God is calling *this* church at *this* time to be and do in *this* place. As Bishop Laurie Green has put it: 'Many parish churches overwhelm themselves with actions, meetings and projects ... which may in fact be a squandering of energies and resources rather than a faithful commitment to engage incarnationally with God in the world.'[2]

Another force that can shape the life of a church is that of internal politics, with strong people wanting to control what is going on. Sometimes they have made major contributions in the past, but now they are holding on to the past (and often many of the posts) in order to make sure that 'nothing changes here'. Power issues of this sort need to be acknowledged and addressed, painful though it often is.

■   *vision*: **develops and communicates a shared sense of where it is going**

This is not primarily about having a Mission Statement, as these can easily mask a lack of vision. That is because a formula of words is sought, with the best of intentions, to embrace everything that is currently being done. So the Mission Statement has the effect of giving permission to carry on just as we were before, but feeling we now know where we are going. Such Statements are rarely remembered.

Not that all Mission Statements are like that. They may give expression to a vision that has developed as a result of prayerful and considered reflection. That is what vision is about. As often as not, it just emerges. Even when it starts with leaders, it does not become real unless owned by most of the church. The best way to achieve that ownership is not to 'sell' a vision but rather to allow and encourage people to design it. They are then much more motivated to work to bring it into being.

■   *mission priorities*: **consciously sets both immediate and long-term goals**

One of the 'unhealthy' ways in which vision and vocation get stuck is that they are left in the abstract as things we are in favour of, but they never become expressed in action or affect what is done. Healthy churches, on the other hand, take their sense of vocation, and their vision, sufficiently seriously to do something about it. Sometimes the action they take is to dare to stop some activity altogether. Certainly stopping for long enough to discern just what it is that God is calling us to, is a sign of health. Frantic activity in a thousand directions is not a good sign in an individual or a church. This is where this mark and the seventh mark (*doing a few things and doing them well*) usually work together. When a church takes time to discern God's call on its life it will end up doing a few things and doing them well. In so doing they demonstrate the validity of Christ's invitation to:

> *Come to me, all you that are weary and are carrying heavy burdens, and I will give you rest. Take my yoke upon you, and learn from me; for I am gentle and humble in heart, and you will find rest for your souls. For my yoke is easy, and my burden is light.*[3]

■ **able to call for, and make, *sacrifices*, personal and corporate, in bringing about the above and living out the faith**

Where there is a sense of vocation and vision people will go beyond the normal and safe limits of giving of time, energy and resources. The stories told above under this mark all involved different forms of sacrifice that individuals and churches were willing to embrace.

Essentially what is happening when this mark is evident in a church is that the church's spirituality (first mark) is engaging with its sense of mission (second mark). By a process of prayerful reflection, a corporate sense of direction emerges and people discover their own sense of vocation within that broader vision.

An illustration of this dynamic of the marks reinforcing each other is the story of a church that spent over 18 months seeking to discover what God was calling them to be and become. They came to a one-word answer, that God was calling them to *hospitality*. They understood this first as being invited, in the Eucharist, to *receive* hospitality from God. They then saw that they were called to offer hospitality to one another ('Welcome one another, therefore, just as Christ has welcomed you')[4] and that that should have a profound impact on the quality of their relationships within the church. They then recognized that they were called to offer hospitality within their local community and focused all their energies into caring for immigrants and other groups that felt excluded by society. They were sometimes criticized in the local community because they were friends with doubtful characters, just as Christ was.

Their faith (first mark) led them to seek God's call upon the life of the church (third mark), which resulted in a deep commitment to the people who were not part of the church (second mark). As is so often the case in practice, these marks do not stand alone but are woven together, with one mark feeding and strengthening others.

Fourth mark: faces the cost of change and growth

Mark 4: faces the cost of change and growth
rather than resisting change and fearing failure

- while embracing the past, it dares to take on *new ways of doing things*
- *takes risks:* admits when things are not working, and learns from experience
- *crises:* responds creatively to challenges that face the church and community
- *positive experiences of change:* however small, are affirmed and built on.

Healthy churches face the cost of change and growth rather than resisting or running from change. They are prepared to take carefully considered risks whilst unhealthy ones fear failure and so dare not act.

The fact is that change is a sign of life and growth: it is also a fact of life. All of us are changing all the time; indeed not a single atom now contributing to the make-up of our physical being was part of our body seven years ago.

However, many misunderstand change, not least in the life of the church and think it means changing some organizational aspect, such as the liturgical form of worship, the times of Sunday services, or the church building. The truth is that real change is a change of heart. As Fullan has said 'changing formal structures is not the same as changing norms, habits, skills, beliefs'.[5] That is what real change is about.

I was once privileged to be one of three consultants working with a UPA church seeking to engage effectively with a seriously disadvantaged community. One of the other consultants was a Catholic nun. At one meeting about six months after we had begun to work with this church the priest expressed frustration about the fact that nothing seemed to work or make any difference. The nun said, 'Brother, you need to understand that real change does not happen on an electrical timescale but a horticultural one.' Real change takes time to grow and develop.

It also requires a willingness to stop and reflect on the value of what we are doing, so this mark connects closely with seeking to find out what God wants, and doing a few things and doing them well. Too easily, both personally and as churches, we rush around in a frenzy of busy-ness bearing little fruit. As Loren Mead has put it: 'busyness is the escape mechanism most people use to avoid the pain of learning and change'.[6]

Some of the ways in which a healthy attitude to change can be seen are as follows:

■ **while embracing the past, it dares to take on *new ways of doing things***

David Ford, Regius Professor of Divinity at Cambridge said at a conference a few years ago: 'our calling is to improvise in ways which surprise and delight and yet ring true with the past'.

Broadly speaking that improvising comes in two shapes, the evolutionary and the revolutionary. It either takes what is and reworks it, or else it seeks to begin again. It is good to be alive to both those options. We see it today in the larger scene of the life of the Church. The evolutionary mode is about the Church operating in *inherited* mode, making 'church as we know it' work in today's changed and changing setting. The revolutionary way is to start with a new group in a new setting and work out together how to nourish and express our faith. Often a combination is required.

A health warning needs to be issued here. Some seemingly 'revolutionary' changes are actually not nearly revolutionary enough. A classic example is a church plant in a local pub. The church thinks it is doing something radical because of where it is meeting, yet how it operates (e.g. the music it uses) remains largely unchanged. In such situations the church has missed a vital opportunity really to 'begin again'.

■ ***takes risks*: admits when things are not working, and learns from experience**

There can be no guarantee of 'success' in this life, so faith often shows itself in a willingness to follow a hunch or conviction.

> One church, aware that no one from a large council estate in the parish came to church, decided to do a 'church plant'

on the estate. Ten people agreed to form the church plant and to report back within three years. When they reported back they had to admit that no one had been added to the life of the church through the church plant so they recommended it be closed. Six months later the local pub was closed and the church seized the opportunity, through a Church Urban Fund grant, to buy the pub and turn it into a youth and community centre. Out of all that, a group of people emerged who wanted to explore the faith. Having done so, they discovered a personal relationship with God, met weekly to pray, worship and support each other. Once a month, the vicar came to take a Eucharist. With hindsight they realized that what had happened, really without their noticing it, was that they had planted a church.

The original church plant 'failed'. Or, did it? Was it not a necessary part on the journey to the forming of the church plant that was a more radical expression than anyone could envisage? It was certainly a healthy church in its attitude to change and can be commended for a whole number of reasons. They were full of courage, for they dared to face the fact that no one from the estate came to church, and to have a go at planting a church. They dared to monitor the situation and not to massage the statistics in doing so. They had the courage to close the church plant without having anything to replace that strategy. Furthermore, they then dared to have another go with the youth and community centre. It is a fine example of a church having the courage and tenacity to face the cost of change and growth.

■   *crises*: **responds creatively to challenges that face the church and community**

Trees and even skyscrapers bend with the wind. Human beings make choices as they adapt to changed circumstances. So too do healthy churches. They are responsive rather than rigid and ploughing on regardless come what may.

Open Doors, Open Minds,[7] is a fine story of a church that had been described as a 'preaching shop' and which saw the pulpit as the focal point in evangelism. But they noticed that the local community contained a growing number of bedsits and an influx of people on benefits, often with drug or relational problems or suffering from mental or emotional disturbance. They came nowhere near the church. Courageously the church faced this fact and did something about it. They reordered the back of the church to create a meeting point where drinks, light refreshments and conversations were available. Unconsciously they thought they had done their part by opening their doors. But, once people from the community started to come for drinks, the church found that the conversations, and indeed the conversions, were two way. Their theology was being challenged. They came to realize that relationships rather than pulpits are the key to communicating the faith today. It was a major learning, and turning, point for the church. Here is creative and costly response to a changing world.

■ *positive experiences of change*: **however small, are affirmed and built on**

Many of the churches whose stories we heard had a track record of good experiences of change. Yet the more striking truth was that many had stories to tell of experiments that came to nothing and good ideas that fell flat. They were able to admit when things were not working and, because of the positive credits in the church's 'memory bank of change', were able to press on rather than give up. For a number of them, starting small and then learning from those positive experiences had been an important pattern.

Sometimes churches have a large debit balance in their 'memory bank of change'. This means that building to a credit balance will take longer. However, one of the ways of doing that is to have out in the open the past negative experience and to explore what the church has learned, or could learn, from those experiences. That can shift painful past experiences from the debit to the credit side of the account.

Listening to the stories of these and many other churches suggests there may be three broad types of church. Some are simply heading in the wrong direction. This will include those churches going nowhere. Others are churches on the journey to health, bearing in mind that health is a journey, not a destination we arrive at. The third type, and there may be many in this category, are those that have been on the journey to health but have become stuck or have ducked some issue without which the journey cannot be resumed.

Three or four decades ago one church was asked to pilot · some new form of Eucharist as part of the Church of England's revision of its liturgy. It was called Series Two. The church was delighted to be in the vanguard of new developments in the life of the church. Sadly, time has passed that church by. It is still using that form of service. It did step out into change, but then it became stuck.

Certainly churches on the journey to health are ones that have come up against costly experiences of pain, puzzlement, change and conflict. In them health is evidenced by their willingness and capacity to face uncomfortable truth and real obstacles, but to keep going. They are the churches that reap the rewards of staying faithful to the costly call to follow Christ.

Chapter 4
Sign of the kingdom

Operates as a community, makes room for all *and* does a few things and does them well

The Church is not only called to tell good news of the coming of God's kingdom and to share in the work of the kingdom here on earth, it is also called to embody the presence of God's reign in human society by the way it orders and expresses its life. As Crosby has put it: 'the church must be the first sign of what it preaches'.[1]

Because of God's trinitarian nature as Three-Persons-in-One, his life will find fullest expression in and through relationships, hence the importance of community and the church operating as one. Yet this is frequently a neglected aspect of the Church's life. So, for example, the Report[2] that set up the Archbishops' Council identified the essential tasks of the Church as being worship, mission and service. Community was not part of the picture and that despite the use of two almost interchangeable words: 'mission' and 'service'. Not surprisingly, Michael Riddell has said: 'Congregations do not generally operate as Christian communities. They are instead gatherings of individuals.'[3]

The last three marks of a healthy church explored in this chapter all point to the Church as a community of faith, which, by the way it orders its whole life, is a living demonstration and 'pilot project' of the kingdom of God.

Fifth mark: operates as a community

Mark 5: operates as a community
rather than functioning as a club or religious organization

■ *relationships:* are nurtured, often in small groups, so that people feel accepted and are helped to grow in faith and service
■ *leadership:* lay and ordained work as a team to develop locally appropriate expressions of all seven marks of a healthy church
■ *lay ministry:* the different gifts, experiences and faith journeys of all are valued and given expression in and beyond the life of the church.

Healthy churches are communities and operate as such rather than as a club or religious organization. Communities put the focus on valuing people for their own sake and for their distinctiveness. They put a high value on establishing and maintaining good personal relationships. Clubs and organizations tend rather to put their attention on communicating unwritten norms of behaviour that make someone acceptable, or not, and on the contribution members make to getting the task done.

Not that life is actually as black and white as that. Communities have a 'job' to be done and good organizations do care about the quality of relationships with their structure. Nonetheless, there is a difference.

There is a particular relevance of this mark in today's culture. People value relationships and want to *belong*, typically doing so in small, informal and fluid networks. They are resistant to *joining* organizations that have a more impersonal, fixed and controlling feel to them.

This means that a church that functions as a community is more likely to engage with people today than a church that operates in organizational mode. Yet, the Church in recent centuries has been slow to understand itself as a community. As John Westerhoff has put it: 'we commonly think of the Christian life from an individualistic or, at best, an organisational perspective, but rarely from a communal one'.[4]

This may well explain the consistent evidence of recent research that small churches are doing better than large ones. Small churches naturally operate as communities (though too easily as 'closed communities'), whilst large ones easily feel like an organization. Not surprisingly, one of the characteristics of flourishing larger churches is that they make considerable use of small groups. They have found ways of building the value of the small into the structure of the large, thus enabling them to operate as a community.

This shows itself in healthy churches in three particular ways.

■ **relationships: are nurtured, often in small groups, so that people feel accepted and are helped to grow in faith and service**

Healthy churches are aware of and take care about relationships. Not only one to one but also in building a sense of community and belonging. This often shows in their capacity to celebrate and party as well as in the way the notices are handled in Sunday services. It usually results in a wide number of people being involved in different ways in the life of the church. That involvement typically will be related to their particular gifts and personality, for communities recognize and release gifts rather than squeeze people into roles they do not fit. It is not a matter of a few people doing everything but of a church that is discovering how to welcome the contribution of a diverse group of people.

> One church had a couple of young men who 'suffered' from Down's syndrome. 'Suffered' was seen in inverted commas because the church recognized ways in which these young men had a remarkable ability to care for people and express love. They were welcomed into the stewarding team that greeted people as they entered church. It was a church that often had prayer for healing at the communion rail after the administration of the sacrament. These two young men were also involved in praying for others. People often commented after being prayed for by them: 'it was pretty clear who really was in their right mind and had grasped the point of life'.

This does not always mean that everything in a church that operates as a community is always sweetness and light. Indeed, one of the ways in which the strength of a community can be measured is by how it handles conflict. As Roberta Bondi has put it:

> *One form of love-destroying dishonesty characteristic of life together in our marriages and churches is our niceness. In our niceness we believe that being supportive means never speaking our real thoughts and feelings in areas of disagreement ... Where we disagree, we need to push against each other in direct ways rather than in underhanded ways that usually result in mutual bitterness.*[5]

■   *leadership*: **lay and ordained work as a team to develop locally appropriate expressions of all seven marks of a healthy church**

Despite the considerable range of personality types evident among the leaders of the churches we met, what was evident was that their style was an enabling one. They were good at affirming the gifts and contribution of all. This is well beyond the one-man (or one-woman) band. Here were people willing to trust and affirm others in the exercise of their ministry. The perspective of these leaders was consistently one of seeing their role as enabling the ministry of the whole church rather than doing the ministry for the whole church themselves. They celebrated the gifts of others rather than felt threatened by them. This can be seen as a shift from a priestly role (in the sense of being *the* person who ministers to the congregation) to an episcopal one (overseeing the ministry of *all*) role taking place in these churches. As John Adair, in his fascinating book about the various approaches to leadership at the time of Christ, puts it, the leader was 'often chosen for his ... generosity or the willingness to put others' needs before his own, and a lack of arrogance'.[6] There is also a shift in the leadership role of such clergy from being providers of answers to the church to formulators of questions that the church needs to address.[7]

■   *lay ministry*: **the different gifts, experiences and faith journeys of all are valued and given expression in and beyond the life of the church**

Put simply, healthy churches are highly participative. People today are less inclined to be passengers or 'pew fodder'. Those whose faith is real want to do something about it and with it. Good churches make that possible.

One of the striking and widespread ways in which this can be observed in a church today is in the work of evangelism, not least in churches that might run a mile from thinking they are doing any such thing.

Even 20 years ago, evangelism was seen as something that a few specialists did – the rest of us got on with other things. Now, however, the Church increasingly sees evangelism as 'helping people on the journey to faith'. Typically this is done through running some 'process evangelism' course such as *Alpha* or *Emmaus* (see *Resources* section for more details). Evangelism now is what *we* do, together. Some of us invite people to the next course; others have skills in leading, in handling discussion, in making meals or refreshments available, in praying for those on the course, in answering people's questions, others in organizing the whole process. We, as a church, are in it together. The church has become the evangelist, and strengthened its sense of community in the process.

Not, as has already been mentioned, that 'lay ministry' is all about 'what I do in church'. Healthy churches, because they have an outward-looking focus, work to affirm people in their daily living and life well beyond the life of the church.

> One church, because of its particular setting in commuter territory was aware that committee work was not just some-thing that happened in church. A considerable number of church members spent a large proportion of their working life in committees. So the church majored on doing committees really well. They thought, read, researched and prayed about it all. They brought in national experts both to speak and to train them in doing committees well. Now church members not only enjoy their church committee work, they can take insights from that experience into their

work situation. The faith community is empowering them for daily living.

Another church focused its energies on developing listening skills in its life. This is not only helping to build the church as a community in which people really do listen to one another, but it has a wider goal too. It is equipping people in their marriages and in their leisure and work situations, as well as in community politics, to make a 'listening contribution' to all they do. They are also finding that evangelism is taking place because people making some tentative contact with the church are finding that their own spiritual journey is being listened to and taken seriously before any attempt is made to explain the Christian faith to them.

Sixth mark: makes room for all

Mark 6: makes room for all
being inclusive rather than exclusive

- *welcome*: works to include newcomers into the life of the church
- *children and young people*: are helped to belong, contribute and be nurtured in their faith
- *enquirers* are encouraged to explore and experience faith in Christ
- *diversities*: different social and ethnic backgrounds, mental and physical abilities, and ages, are seen as a strength.

Healthy churches make room for all. They are inclusive rather than exclusive, though this is so much easier to write than practise.

- ### *welcome*: works to include newcomers into the life of the church

We have noted a whole range of levels of response to the work of welcome, as follows, beginning with the least effective and working up to the most wholesome:

- some churches consider themselves welcoming because *everyone who is currently 'in'* the church feels at home there. Such churches have not stopped to see how things look from 'outside' existing membership. Becoming part of a church can prove daunting, so potential newcomers conclude that they are not wanted there. That may well be the case.

- other churches do welcome some newcomers, but within a narrow band. These churches want *more people like us*, but have subtle and effective ways of freezing out anyone who looks, dresses, or sounds different from us.

- there are churches that *talk a good talk about welcome*. 'Newcomers are warmly invited to join us for coffee afterwards' says the vicar in the notices. But in practice they are not. Regular church members huddle in their own groups while visitors are left to fend for themselves.

- then there are churches that *give a real verbal welcome*. You will be greeted at the door, shown to a seat, even introduced to one or two members of the church who will say, genuinely, 'hello, its nice to see you'. The problem here is that no one seems to know what to say after they have said 'hello'. Real welcome is what happens *after* we have said 'hello'.

- a further group of churches does welcome newcomers not only to the services, but also to church activities, but the welcome *is to be part of the audience*. We would like more people to buy things at the bring-and-buy, more to hear our choir sing at the annual festival, but that is really as far as we want newcomers to enter the church.

- finally there are the churches that *incorporate newcomers*. This is a costly task for it means making others part of our life, allowing the warmth of the friendships we enjoy to be taken, broken open, blessed and given to others with whom the only thing we may feel we have in common is our faith in Christ. It may take a while to realize that our common humanity is something we also share – and find enriched by our very differences. These churches also are willing to let others participate in the life of the church. They do so joyfully aware that, like a couple welcoming their first child into their shared life, that major changes will inevitably be required. Here we come across the two great commandments again, for, as Raymond Fung has put it, 'love of God & others is not just the church's foreign policy it's its domestic policy too'.[8]

One church did a PCC day in which they went through the marks of a healthy church, scored their own church and identified four things that they needed to work on. One of the four items that had been identified as needing attention was 'Welcome'. In the afternoon session the 16 members of the PCC were about to choose which of the four groups each exploring one of these themes they wanted to join. The vicar suggested to the facilitator that 'it would be good if we could have four of us in each group'. Temptingly tidy though the suggestion was, the person facilitating the event resisted this in favour of letting people choose to work with whatever mattered to them – even if all 16 went in one group. The PCC members divided in three groups. Those groups were of fairly equal size. The one topic that had no one wanting to work on it, was ... *Welcome*! It was a most instructive moment for them as they realized that, although this needed attending to, none of them wanted to address the issue. Subsequent to that day, they did go away and work on it. Their motivation to do so came largely from that eye-opening experience of realizing that it was an issue they all wanted to leave to someone else.

A number of years ago, the Pentecostal Church in South America did some research into why some people who started coming to church only came for a few weeks and then stopped whilst others became full and long-term members. They came up with a simple principle about the importance of forming significant relationships with people who were already members. The statistics were quite stark. Of those newcomers who formed a significant relationship with six members of the church in their first six months of attending that church, 98 per cent stayed. For those who made no significant relationship, only 2 per cent stayed. The percentage of those who stayed went up steadily for every one significant relationship that a newcomer made. That is the heart of welcome, opening our hearts, ourselves and our lives to others.

■ *children and young people*: **are helped to belong, contribute and be nurtured in their faith**

Our society today is much less connected between generations. People relate more within fairly narrow age bands. The gospel calls us to reach out across those divides. Certainly, churches that do so engage are significantly more likely to be churches to which people are attracted.

There is a danger here of engaging in wishful thinking. Churches that have no one under 60 years old sometimes express an ardent desire 'to have young people in this church'. However, this can easily be a pipe dream rather than a vision. What they would actually like is for children and young people to join us in *what we are already doing* – but staying quiet and attentive whilst doing so. They certainly would not want to change anything simply because children and young people were present. That would not be joining, just attending.

Such a church would be better off not wishing for the (conveniently) unattainable, but starting to work for (the more disturbingly) possible, namely that the church starts to grow younger. So, if there is no one under 60, the task is so to change how we operate as to attract people in their 50s. Once we start getting answers there we can move on to ask the same question about how we can really welcome the 40-year-olds. By the time we have incorporated the 30-year-olds we will be having to cope with teenagers and young people come what may. Healthy churches make sure they are aiming at honest, realistic and achievable goals.

■ *enquirers*: **are encouraged to explore and experience faith in Christ**

The first mark of a healthy church, that it is energized by faith, finds expression in the nurturing of the faith of its members – rather than assuming faith. These churches see the faith as providing 'resources for living' and set out to find ways of doing that for their members. A natural development of this is that such churches also do the same for those enquiring about the faith. That enquiry may take the form of asking direct questions about what Christians believe, but is more likely to be in the form of a much less articulated desire to 'make sense of life'.

One of the most obvious things that such churches have spotted is that the typical Sunday service is not necessarily the best or right place for an enquirer to start, simply for the reason that the one thing they want to do is ask questions, and that rarely fits with most public acts of worship. So wise churches develop ways into membership appropriate for the people with whom they have contact.[9]

■ *diversities*: **different social and ethnic backgrounds, mental and physical abilities, and ages, are seen as a strength**

In earlier forms of this mark the wording used was *makes room for others*. Some who had been practising this mark for years pointed out the danger of the terminology. The point they made was that, if we see different groups as 'others' in an 'us/them' dynamic, then any incorporation will be partial. Although they find a place in the church, they will remain 'the others'. This is why we changed to the present wording to communicate this sense of the church as a rich and diverse community, held together by the love of God and one another rather than by any limited socially shared background we might have in common.

In the research on which *Hope for the Church* [10] is based, it was discovered that churches that had some engagement with young people, churches that had an ethnic mix and churches that were using the *Alpha* course, were all more likely to be growing than the average church. The view Bob Jackson, as a statistician, took was that these three were symptomatic of a deeper truth about these churches. They all had clearly developed the ability to incorporate people who are 'not like us': people, that is, of a different age, from a difference ethnic grouping and people who were not currently churchgoers. Churches that are able to embrace such diversity are more likely to grow simply because there are more doors through which people can enter the life of the church.

Seventh mark: does a few things and does them well

Mark 7: does a few things and does them well
focused rather than frenetic

- *does the basics well*: especially public worship, pastoral care, stewardship and administration
- *occasional offices*: make sense of life and communicate faith
- *being good news* as a church in its attitudes and ways of working
- *enjoys what it does* and is relaxed about what is not being done.

This is the mark that most surprised us and uncovered in us an unconscious assumption that growing churches were simply churches running faster than others, being more energetic and active than most other churches. What we discovered was very different. Here were churches and people relaxed and comfortable with what they were doing. They were *focused rather than frantic*, able to leave some things undone, able to enjoy life and all that is and to reflect on the value of what they are doing.

In the course of communicating these marks we came across an instructive misreading of this one. Some had thought we were saying that healthy churches 'do a few things well ... *but most of what they do is pretty ordinary*'. That was not what we saw or meant.

Some of the ways in which this mark is evident are as follows:

■ ***does the basics well*: especially public worship, pastoral care, stewardship and administration**

These churches were not primarily distinguished by doing extraordinary things or by doing a vast number of different things, but by doing a quality job with the basic things. Church buildings were tidy and uncluttered, meetings were well run, thought was put into the leading of worship and to care of individuals. The administration of these churches does not draw attention to itself but the job, whether the PCC minutes, the Sunday notices sheet, or the handling of the finances and proper attention to tax rebates on covenanted giving, were all likely to be done well. 'Quietly efficient' seems to be their style.

■ ***occasional offices*: make sense of life and communicate faith**

Here is a further place where this mark shows itself. Baptisms, weddings, funerals, and the preparation for them, are done well. They are unhurried, with thought, care and attention to detail and done in a loving and prayerful way that establishes good relationships with those involved. The goal was to do a quality job.

■ ***being good news*: as a church in its attitudes and ways of working**

Healthy churches recognize that they are called to proclaim the good news of Jesus Christ by how they are church, usually long before they have any opportunity to speak about faith to people personally.

The dynamic we observed was that, in these churches, because people were not frantically trying to do too much, they did a few things well, which gave them great satisfaction. As a result, much of what they do tends to have a genuinely positive effect because it is a quality job. Doing a good job not only brings its own reward, it also – usually – has a positive effect (e.g. adding to the numbers attending or the positive responses made).

In contrast, in other churches, too much is taken on, done in a rushed and slapdash way (there is not the time to do more), so what is done does not really work. The result of this approach is that the feeling is 'if only we did a few more things' all would be well. In truth the answer is to do less and do it better, but that seems far removed from the culture of such churches. Such churches do find that 'My yoke is easy and my burden light'. This is where *seeking to find out what God wants* often bears fruit. A quiet sense of vocation pervades the whole church.

Churches have addressed this. It takes time to develop this mark. Some have helped by encouraging people to take on just one task in the church and do that well, but this involves considerable change and letting go of perceived 'essential services'. Because it involves a culture change within the church it is wise to reckon that significant progress might well take several years.

■ *enjoys what it does* and is relaxed about what is not being done

There is a significantly higher sense of enjoying church in healthy churches. Christian Schwarz, in *Natural Church Development*[11] notes that laughter is one of the marks of a healthy church. One could add 'and tears', for healthy churches have an attractive and real humanity and are not trying to impress or achieve. They are what they preach. It is that simple – and that costly.

> A flourishing rural church was eager to communicate its faith but wanted to do it in a way that both connected with the surrounding community and that did not leave themselves with an overloaded programme or unachievable goals. They decided to hold four *Food for Thought* evenings each year in the village hall. A very good meal was laid on and tables were beautifully laid and decorated. Each evening they had someone with an interesting job who came to speak about their work and their faith. The vicar reported that his primary job after the first couple of years was persuading church members not to attend so that those who did not go to church could have a place, since seats were sold out several weeks in advance. It was clearly done very well, with a great sense of occasion. They were very enjoyable evenings and a means of provoking a steady stream of people wanting to explore the faith further. At Christmas over one third of the total population of the three villages attended church on Christmas Eve or Christmas Day.

So this exploration of these seven marks brings us back to where we began. Healthy churches live out a faith that is real to them and shapes what they do and how they do it.

The Seven Marks of a Healthy Church
expressing the life of Christ through the local church

Mark 1: energized by faith

rather than just keeping things going or trying to survive

- *worship and sacramental life*: move people to experience God's love
- *motivation*: energy comes from a desire to serve God and one another
- *engages with Scripture*: in creative ways that connect with life
- *nurtures faith in Christ*: helping people to grow in, and share, their faith.

Mark 2: outward-looking focus

with a 'whole life' rather than a 'church life' concern

- deeply rooted in the *local community*, working in partnership with other denominations, faiths, secular groups and networks
- passionate and prophetic about *justice and peace*, locally and globally
- makes connections between *faith and daily living*
- responds to human need by *loving service*.

Mark 3: seeks to find out what God wants

discerning the Spirit's leading rather than trying to please everyone

- *vocation*: seeks to explore what God wants it to be and do
- *vision*: develops and communicates a shared sense of where it is going
- *mission priorities*: consciously sets both immediate and long-term goals
- able to call for, and make, *sacrifices*, personal and corporate, in bringing about the above and living out the faith.

Mark 4: faces the cost of change and growth

rather than resisting change and fearing failure

- while embracing the past, it dares to take on *new ways of doing things*
- *takes risks*: admits when things are not working, and learns from experience

- *crises*: responds creatively to challenges that face the church and community
- *positive experiences of change*: however small, are affirmed and built on.

Mark 5: operates as a community

rather than functioning as a club or religious organization

- *relationships*: are nurtured, often in small groups, so that people feel accepted and are helped to grow in faith and service
- *leadership*: lay and ordained work as a team to develop locally appropriate expressions of all seven marks of a healthy church
- *lay ministry*: the different gifts, experiences and faith journeys of all are valued and given expression in and beyond the life of the church.

Mark 6: makes room for all

being inclusive rather than exclusive

- *welcome*: works to include newcomers into the life of the church
- *children and young people*: are helped to belong, contribute and be nurtured in their faith
- *enquirers* are encouraged to explore and experience faith in Christ
- *diversities*: different social and ethnic backgrounds, mental and physical abilities, and ages, are seen as a strength.

Mark 7: does a few things and does them well

focused rather than frenetic

- *does the basics well*: especially public worship, pastoral care, stewardship and administration
- *occasional offices*: make sense of life and communicate faith
- *being good news* as a church in its attitudes and ways of working
- *enjoys what it does* and is relaxed about what is not being done.

(A photocopiable version of this summary is given in Appendix 4, for use in the Church Profile Exercise.)

Part 2:
Growing healthy churches

Chapter 5
Embarking on the healthy journey

A few years ago my wife and I went for a stroll through some woods along what we thought was a level path. Soon after we set out the path began to drop down a defile and we began to hear the sound of lapping water. Before long we were in a hidden valley walking alongside a beautiful quiet lake completely hidden from the surrounding world and framed in great banks of rhododendrons in full flower. It was a wonderful sight and a complete surprise. Talking to a local farmer on the way back, we discovered that the lake had been created a century earlier by a wealthy landowner. It was a twenty-first birthday present for his daughter. That experience of surprise, discovery and adventure is what makes walking so enjoyable.

Churches seeking to develop their health also experience it as a journey full of discovery and a sense of adventure. What this chapter sets out is an overview of that journey before we engage with the first stage of the journey in the next chapter, namely the Church Profile Exercise. Because that exercise can be done at a single meeting it could give the impression that that is how long it takes to develop the health of a church, which is why we need first to stand back in order to grasp the bigger picture of the journey to health.

The transforming pilgrimage

'Healthy Churches' is definitely not a quick fix or a programme as such, but rather about a settled determination, whatever the false turns and setbacks may be, to develop the health of the church. Experience suggests that a church working with this approach is likely to take eighteen months to two years to identify its present strengths and weaknesses, decide where action is needed, take that action and review progress made.

So becoming a healthy church is rather like a journey, but a particular journey, a pilgrimage. For the journey into greater health is a journey both with and towards the presence of God. While tourists typically want to get to their destination, the pilgrim knows that making the journey is as much part of the goal as is arriving. That is certainly true about the marks of a healthy church. One of the best ways of becoming a healthy church is by seeking to live out the marks *in the very way* in which we set about seeking the health of the church. So how the process is managed needs careful attention. *Doing a few things and doing them well* certainly applies here, as does the need for the whole process to be *energized by faith* and grounded in *seeking to find out what God wants*.

Here are some of the ways in which we can practise these marks as we work to discern the health of a church and to develop its life.

Energized by faith: Make the whole matter a subject for prayer both in the intercessions in church and by encouragement in personal and group prayer. This can be aided by producing a single sheet of prayer suggestions on the subject with some specific things to do, some things to reflect on and one or two prayers to pray.

Outward-looking focus: Have a suggestions box and invite people to keep their eyes and ears open for other churches that might have something to teach us, workplaces that may have been wrestling with this issue, books, stories, people, passages from Scripture, any of which might speak to us. This can help lift our eyes beyond our immediate setting and help us to see the wider world in a new light.

Seeks to find out what God wants: Putting the issue in the form 'what do you think that God might want us to do about this issue?' shifts the agenda and provokes people to look at it in a new way.

Faces the cost of change and growth: Just the idea that we need to do something about some aspect of the life of the church assumes that things could be improved, which will necessarily involve change. A change dynamic is being set up simply by the whole church's being invited to think about the matter and come up with ideas.

Operates as a community: This approach, because everyone is being counted in and everyone's contribution is welcomed, gives expression to the fact that 'we are all in this together' and that our being a community matters more than any decision-making hierarchy that may exist. A church council exists to serve the community of faith not to usurp its life and vitality. This sense of 'all being in this together' is a great way to build community in the life of the church.

Inviting as wide a group as possible, indeed the whole church membership (with no upper or lower age limit), to come up with ideas about what would help will be much more likely to connect with them than some plan imposed from above. Giving such an open invitation also 'shakes the leadership tree' by making plans for future development something that the whole church is involved in shaping.

One church decided to take a new look at the whole of church life. Everyone was encouraged to be in a short-term neighbourhood group in order to develop plans that were 'grassroots up' rather than 'top-down' plans. Over one hundred new members have been added to that church in the last six years. There is a connection between those last two sentences!

Makes room for all: The very fact of opening up the issue to the whole church both robs the power operators of their control of the 'levers of power' and also empowers many voices that are not usually listened to. It is surprising where ideas may bubble up from. What is certain is that such a process is likely to stimulate participation by a wider group of people. The wider the group of people involved in *designing* our plans for addressing the issue in question, the greater is the likelihood that they will want to be part of the *implementing* of anything that emerges as our next step in this matter.

Does a few things and does them well: Simply focusing on this one issue and doing so as a whole church signals and practises this matter of focusing on one task at a time. Consulting widely within the church is more likely to produce a quality plan than any rushed discussion and decision at a church council alone – though at some stage they will have an important decision-making role to fulfil.

Mapping the path for individual churches

So developing the health of a church is a long-term process we need to engage with if we are to see any fruit. Furthermore, the very way in which we set about that can either build, or destroy, the very marks of a healthy church we are seeking to develop. With that as background we turn now to an outline of the steps along the way of the healthy churches process, which are as follows.

Phase one: *diagnosis – with the Church Profile Exercise*

This three-hour process is outlined in detail in the next chapter. It is designed to be done with either a church leadership group (such as the church council) or with a whole church meeting. Some churches have used both approaches and then reflected on any differences of scoring between the two *profiles* that emerge.

The exercise begins with an introduction of the seven marks of a healthy church, during which participants are asked to score the church on a scale of 1 (low) to 6 (high) for each mark. At the end of that, all the individual scores are transposed onto a large flipchart sheet so a corporate profile of the church can be read off.

Once a *church profile* has been developed then the group can begin to reflect on the patterns that emerge in that profile. This is done initially in a general way by looking at three areas. First, identifying *strengths* that are suggested by the profile. Churches sometimes find it difficult to accept that their church could be good at *anything*. It is one of the important things that a facilitator can do: help the church own and celebrate its strengths.

The next area of the profile to explore is where there are significant *divergences* in scorings. These can often be very revealing. Sometimes they show two aspects of the same mark, such as one church where some people scored 'Energized by faith' high, while another group scored it low. When invited to say why they had scored the church 'high' or 'low' what emerged was as follows. Those scoring the church 'high' pointed to the number of home groups and prayer groups in the church. Those scoring 'low' pointed to the fact that less than half of those attending Sunday services were involved in anything like that. Sometimes 'divergences' reflect the fact that there is a wide range of opinion in the church on the subject and yet the matter has never been addressed. These are sometimes the important things the church needs to address rather than avoid.

A further area to explore is *things that are holding us back*. Christian Schwarz, in *Natural Church Development*,[1] has a helpful illustration here. He uses the image of a water barrel or tub made of vertical staves of wood. He points out that, if the staves are of different height, then water can only fill the barrel to the top of the lowest stave. After that, however much water is poured in, it will drain away. The key is obviously to raise the height of the lowest staves.

What is being explored at this stage is where there are any perceived weaknesses in the life of the church. It takes courage to own, face and address weaknesses. A healthy church dares to do just that.

Once the general areas of strength, divergence and weakness have been explored, the exercise moves on to identify where action is most needed and what action is most likely to yield positive fruits. Work is done to generate a range of possibilities. This is as far as the Church Profile Exercise takes a church.

It needs to be recognized that this is only the very first step in the journey to health. It is more a matter of orienteering, identifying the right direction, rather than setting out on the journey itself. This is why doing the Church Profile Exercise must not be thought of as in any sense 'doing healthy churches'. Vital steps lie ahead, as follows.

Phase two: *decision by the church leadership group*

Stimulating though most churches find the Church Profile Exercise, time is needed to reflect on the experience and identify the key issues that emerge. Any church embarking on this initial exercise needs to have scheduled in, a few weeks after the exercise, a meeting of whatever leadership group (such as church council) is responsible for taking matters further. This will involve both sharing responses to the exercise event and insights gained in the light of it.

Then work needs to be done to identify the key actions to take. Here it is helpful to narrow down the focus to one, or two at the most, of the marks. This will have become evident during the Church Profile Exercise.

The work now is as follows. It is a great help first of all to list as large a number of options for action as possible. This generating of ideas works best if none of the ideas are explored and no discussion (other than necessary clarification) take places *at this point*. The first task is simply to identify possible options and actions, however crazy they might seem.

Once a reasonable list of options has been developed *then* they can be evaluated. It will soon appear that some go together, others are good but need to be part of a bigger plan and yet others conflict with each other. It will also become clear which ideas are likely to work here. Does it fit this situation? Do we have anyone with the vision and gifts to lead such an action?

After looking at the various options, the leadership group then needs to decide what is going to be done, who is going to do it, with what resources and support they are going to be furnished and in what timescale they are going to monitor progress in this area. It is not sufficient to have a 'good idea' or even 'noble intentions', what is needed here is a specific and achievable action plan.

It is strongly recommended that churches proceed a step at a time. So, for example, if the goal is to communicate the faith to young people in the area, the ideas people come up with may include strengthening links with local schools, reordering the buildings so young people have somewhere to meet, developing a youth leadership team, appointing a youth worker (full-time or part-time), or detached youth worker, inviting the area church youth officer to come to give advice, and to start a Saturday morning youth club. What would be foolish would be to attempt all these at the same time. One step at a time, carefully, thoroughly and joyfully taken is likely to result in greater progress than rushing off in several directions all at the same time. It is a much better policy to decide which one needs to be addressed first, take action on that, and then consider further action in due course, when the first step is already well under way.

Phase three: *action and development*

The next task is to take action as planned, monitoring progress along the way. This may well take the best part of a year before any sort of assessment can be made about whether or not taking these actions has achieved what the church was hoping for. It often proves necessary to revise plans (sometimes even changing them substantially) in the light of experience.

Celebrating is an important part of pilgrimage. Although the church will not have achieved all its goals within a year, there should, nonetheless, be some good things to celebrate and it is important to build these in along the way. Doing so gives expression to a number of the marks of a healthy church. The 'next steps' phase may well involve returning to the Church Profile Exercise with a view to doing the whole exercise again and identifying, in the new circumstances, what are the key issues to work on *now*.

Steps for groups of churches

Where groups of churches are considering working with the healthy churches material there are a number of additional matters that they need to be aware of and give attention to.

This material, as with any such material, works best where people and churches choose freely to do it rather than feel it is required of them (though one diocese did do just that with seemingly very few resisting or doing so reluctantly). More normally, a group of churches takes on something like this because they have been consulted and have decided they want to be counted in.

There then needs to be good publicity for the Church Profile Exercise. This is often done for three to five people from each church, plus incumbent, as a 'taster', with each church then going home and doing it with as many members of the church as can be gathered together, and with the help of a facilitator.

Where it is intended to make facilitators available, they need to be identified, invited, trained and ready for action before any church is at the stage of doing the exercise.

Opportunities for mutual learning, such as a yearly or half-year follow-on day can be of great help to encourage learning to continue.

Where the group is a relatively large one, such as a diocese, it is very valuable for a conscious effort to be made to build the marks of a healthy church into the character and lifestyle of that grouping.

The Way of Christ

Having used the seven marks and worked with churches in the light of them, an intriguing question has arisen. It is this. Why are *these* the marks that are needed to grow a healthy church? Our conclusion has been that it has to do with the fact that they are a reflection of the life of Christ.

He was energized by faith, had an outward-looking focus in life, and sought to find out what God wanted of him. Christ lived his whole life seeking to bring about change in the lives of both individuals and social structures. He drew his disciples into a small group that operated as a community. By the way he reached out to the 'untouchables' of his day, Christ made room for all and, because of his seeking of the Father's will, he did a few things and did them well.

So behind all these marks is the primary call of the Church to express in its own life something of the life of Christ. When the Church responds to that call people around it see something of the life of Christ and are attracted to him, in and through the church. This leads to a further implication.

If these marks are true of Christ, then they are also true of his disciples. Through baptism we are committed to living a life that is energized by faith, expressing love through an outward-looking focus on others and the world around us. In baptism we dedicate ourselves to find out what God wants and face the cost of change and growth involved in doing that. In following Christ we are called to be in communion with fellow disciples. In and beyond that community the disciple is called to reflect Christ's generous and open-hearted welcome, making room for all. Finally, as we seek God's will and live out our faith, we are not to become driven people but rather to live out of a sense of vocation in the whole of life by doing a few things and doing them well.

So these marks point us both to the life of Christ and remind us of our vocation. Individually and as a faith community we are called to express the life of Christ. In doing so we find not only the presence and blessing of God but our own and our church's wholeness.

Chapter 6
Developing healthy churches

Knowing what the marks of a healthy church are is instructive. Doing the Church Profile Exercise and identifying the strengths and weaknesses of a church is usually both fun and fruitful. But, in the final issue, what matters is *taking action* to develop the life and health of a church. All the rest is preliminary.

The question this chapter now addresses is what can be done once any particular mark emerges as needing attention? Outlined below are some of the steps that can be taken to strengthen any of the marks.

Becoming proactive

'The journey of a thousand miles begins with a single step', which makes the first step very important, since we could be stepping out in the wrong direction.

For some churches this is actually a radical step, for church life easily lapses into little more than keeping things going as before. When this happens, the church and its leadership are operating in *reactive mode*, dealing simply with what life throws at them. This is an unhealthy state that ultimately results in a loss of a sense of direction or integrity.

Once we take a decision to address a particular aspect of the life of the church we have shifted into *proactive mode*. Just saying 'we need to work on this aspect of the church's life' can itself be a major step towards health because it indicates this shift into healthy, proactive mode.

Changing church culture

An important principle to grasp is that real change is about changing the culture and spirit of a church, not just its programmes and activities. The goal is to change, in some measure, how we understand and experience God, how we relate to one another and how we engage with the world around us. It means that, in considering where action needs to be taken, we should keep in mind changes in attitudes, values and priorities rather than simply organizational change.

> *'The attitude of the church was opened up; from a secretive, private chapel to being determined to welcome all who came.'*

> *'The church changed from an insular group who thought they knew all the answers to a refreshingly open group who learned to cope well living with all sorts of questions and uncertainty.'*

> *'We were very penny-pinching and honestly tight-fisted. It has taken eleven years but we give away not just money, but a whole attitude of welcome and generosity.'*

'Sticking at it' is going to be important. In our quick-fix, short-attention-span culture it is not easy to do that, but it is a sign of health.

Plotting the starting point

After 22 years in one place my wife and I moved house three times in six years. One of our regrets has been that we did not do a good job of taking photographs of each house and garden *when we arrived there*. We know things changed – for the better – but we had no record of the starting point. The same is true of churches and the life of a faith community. It can be a real help to devise a questionnaire for everyone in the church to fill in at the start of the process.

Something that can help here is devising a questionnaire that will reveal where we are at before we take any new action. For a start it means that we need to identify the outcomes we might be looking for in the development of this mark. So, for example, if a church is wanting to be more consciously *energized by faith*, it will need to ask what would be happening and what would be the evidences of it that we would wish to see?

Here are some possible outcomes of addressing that particular mark:

- More people engaging in personal prayer.
- More people involved in one of the church prayer groups.
- More people speaking naturally about ways in which they have experienced the presence of God in their lives.
- A greater range of prayer groups being formed in the church.
- Prayer being a more obvious and central part of groups such as the church council, choir, parent-and-toddler groups, etc.

- Running a prayer school (a one-day event or weekly series of meetings).
- Information about retreats being more readily available.
- A more widespread use of spiritual directors within the church.
- People being encouraged to go on retreat and actually doing so.

The important thing about the above list is not the individual ideas themselves but the fact that they indicate it is possible to measure even something like being energized by faith. Each church would need to create its own list of *desired outcomes* related to the particular mark it judges needs attention. The above list is simply an example to help develop such a list of *desired and measurable outcomes*.

One use of such a list would be to develop a questionnaire for each member of church to complete, identifying how far the elements listed are currently part of their experience. One of the best ways of doing this is to keep the questionnaire to one side of paper and handing it out during a service when the subject (in this case, being *energized by faith*) is being specifically addressed. In this way everyone in church that day will have completed one. Those not present may well hear about it and ask if they can have a form too. These questionnaires will give indications of where the church is at in this area of its life. That is an important ingredient in deciding what needs working on.

The secret is in finding a way of making such questionnaires straightforward, specific and short. Church members often have experience of developing such questionnaires and it is important, for them and the church, that their skills are recognized and made use of. Such a questionnaire approach works in starting to tackle *any* of the marks.

Identifying the area for action

The marks are the obvious starting points for identifying what needs working on. The whole Church Profile Exercise will raise issues needing to be addressed. Once having identified one or two marks needing attention, the leadership group then should look at the bullet points under those marks and see if they express where effort should be put.

However, sometimes none of the bullet points really expresses the issue that people have been talking about. Here it will be necessary to find our own words to express the issue that needs addressing. Indeed, it may be felt that something that does not come under any of the marks is what matters most. In that case it is important for such a church to work on what has been identified and not worry about the fact that it does not fit the healthy churches scheme. Go with what is judged to be the important issue by those involved in the life of the church.

One way to set about identifying what needs to be done is to work with the church council or church leadership. Ask people to form groups of three and to identify *strengths and weaknesses* as they see them in the life of the church. Then, one issue at a time, get the groups to come up with *suggested options*. With a flipchart and someone ready to write up single words or phrases it should be possible to list a considerable range of ideas and options.

Working with a facilitator

There is great value in having some external facilitator to help in developing the health of a church. Their task is to manage the process, stimulate reflection and conversation and assist in deciding what action should be taken.

They bring expertise, a more objective view of the situation and an ability to give affirmation. The latter usually surprises people, as they expect anyone who looks likes an 'expert' will 'tell us where we are going wrong'. Yet what often happens is that someone outside the situation can see the strengths and is able to affirm them more easily than those closely involved with the life of the church.

Also, someone outside the immediate context is well placed to offer objective advice, steer a group to look at the key issues and point to resources (people as well as programmes and courses) that may be of help.

Their presence adds another very helpful ingredient.

Inviting such a person to work with a church also provokes that church to stick at the process until results begin to emerge. Knowing that the next meeting with a facilitator is taking place shortly has a wonderful focusing effect. Such visits provoke thought about 'successes' and 'struggles' that need reporting. That adds the vital element of monitoring into the situation, which further helps the process forward. The next chapter deals with the work of facilitation more fully.

Keeping a diary of events

This is by no means everyone's cup of tea. It certainly is not a good idea to get anyone to handle this if they are not happy to do so, nor is it essential.

However, a surprising number of people do keep diaries and it is certainly worth asking, for example in a church council or more widely in the church, if anyone would be willing to do this. It can be helpful in plotting the major steps, including setbacks, on the church's current journey. In it a record can be kept of progress made, problems encountered, obstacles not yet overcome, questions being currently addressed and lessons learned. So, for example, a church working on developing the church's expression of having an *outward-looking focus*, might have in its diary:

- Notes from the original discussions that identified this as the issue needing to be addressed and why it was thought to be so.
- Dates when specific matters were discussed, decided upon and action taken.
- References to helpful quotations, books and other resources.
- A note of other churches that members of the church have heard about that might have something helpful to share with us on the subject.
- A note of difficulties encountered and of ways being pursued to overcome, or find a way round, them.
- Any statistical evidence to show what progress, or otherwise, is being made.
- A record of meetings with a consultant, and with any other groups in the local community who might have been invited to give help and time.
- Details of specific plans, timescales, outcomes and who was going to be responsible for taking agreed actions.
- Scripture passages that have become key texts for us in addressing this mark.
- A short, accessible reading list of books people have found helpful in stimulating thinking and action on the subject.
- Study material on the theme suitable for use in small groups.
- Stories that have become part of the story of the church.

So many of these things seem obvious, and hardly worth noting at the time, but we quickly lose so much if we do not keep a record of what is happening.

It is almost always right for the diarist to be someone other than the vicar or church leader. What is needed is someone in the know about what is going on in the life of the church, yet also someone who is reflective and can identify key factors and insights at work.

Raising awareness

Addressing any of the marks of a healthy church will involve the management of change. The sort of change needed to develop any of the marks involves shifting the focus, attitude and spirit within the life of the church. To do that requires a sustained approach that is communicated through as many different means as possible. Some communications experts have suggested that someone needs to hear about something in six different ways before it is likely to lodge in their consciousness. Here are some ways that any issue can be brought to a church's attention.

- Addressing the issue in Sunday services; through *preaching*, notices, *intercessions*;
- Writing *articles* in the church magazine or newssheet;
- Making some *visual display* on a noticeboard in church;
- *Interviewing* people in Sunday services (just before the intercessions) about their experience of how this mark is happening (here or elsewhere);
- Providing *study material* for small groups;
- Creating a *prayer card* on the subject;
- Finding ways to *engage with children and young people* and their ideas on the subject;
- *Talking* about the issues informally;
- Putting the subject on the *church council agenda*;
- Finding some *phrase* that sums up what the issue is about.

Communication needs to come at people from a number of different directions if they are to give proper attention to what is being addressed.

One step at a time

Massive five-year plans are now associated with discredited totalitarian state bureaucracies. They are very much out of fashion. That is good news. It means we do not need to develop some complicated plan to keep us going until the Second Coming. Much simpler, and in the long run more effective, is taking a 'one step at a time' approach – small focused steps that are sufficiently clear that we can know when we have achieved them are what works best. Those steps tend to open up next steps too.

One vicar was eager to do what is a called a Future Search[1] for the local community. This involved getting 64 people from the community to come together for a Thursday evening, whole of Friday and the Saturday morning. He achieved remarkable things, getting a senior police officer, doctor, fire officer, together with a group of teenagers from the local school, district nurse, dentist, undertaker and a good number of representative members of the community and local council together for such a sustained period. It worked very well.

It immediately raised two contrasting new issues. One was resistance in the church to the fact that the vicar was spending all his time (not actually true) in the community instead of getting on with 'church work'. The other was that new people started joining the church, because they had seen its connection with everyday life.

There was need for plenty of reflection on what church is all about and a real work of assimilating newcomers who perhaps had a different (and fresher) understanding of what church and the Christian faith are all about.

Equally, for example, if a church wanted to work on *making room for all* or *operates as a community*, it might hold a weekend away or some church parties at which people could get to know one another across the normal divides that exist both in society and in the church. Addressing the matter of being *energized by faith*, a church might hold a retreat day. Developing an *outward-looking focus* might begin with a community survey.

None of the above examples will get a church all the way but each might help it take a first step. Often it is the first step that is the most difficult.

Each time steps are taken, three things can be done to enhance the value of that step. One is to *celebrate* what has been achieved. Do not wait to change the world before you celebrate, just have plenty of celebrations on the journey. For example, if you are doing a community survey, why not plan to bring all the forms back in on a certain Sunday and express thanksgiving for what you have done? That will be enriched if one or two people are invited to share briefly what they have gained from being involved.

Another action to take after each step is to reflect on what we have learned and achieved: in other words to *monitor* progress. Healthy churches dare to stop, dare to ask difficult questions, dare to admit when things do not work and dare to learn from their mistakes.

A third option is the most difficult. It is about *admitting when some action has not worked*. It is painful, and disappointing, but it usually leads on to good things. Certainly it is much better to say 'it did not work' than to try to raise everyone's spirits by pretending how wonderful it is when everyone knows it was a bit of a flop. Some of the best things in churches have arisen as a result of someone having a go, seeming to fail, but learning from their experience and moving on.

> A small group in a church decided that they wanted to do a parenting course, not just for church members but for everyone in the community who might be interested. They planned it all carefully, advertised it in different places ... and nobody turned up. Determined to run such a course they took a different approach ... with the same result: no one came. They would not give up but did take their time to think about how to set up such a course. A seeming 'chance conversation' about it with the local headteacher produced an offer to let them show a five-minute clip from a video about a parenting course at one of the Parents' Evenings at the local school. Over a dozen couples signed up there and then and they have not looked back since.

We should neither be surprised nor defeated by seeming failure. From it we can learn much about ourselves, about what the real issues are, and about how we can be more effective in the future. 'A church or congregation that moves ahead must be ready to value its failures, to expect many things not to work.'[2] This is not a mark of failure – that we 'got it wrong' – but rather a sign of health – that we are adapting speedily and are able to be honest about what works and what does not work.

What is important to avoid is pretending things worked when they did not, or just giving up rather than learning and pressing on.

The cost of it all

Taking the above steps is costly. Smiling sweetly, saying something soothing or changing the subject are much easier. But they all duck the central issue of addressing issues with courageous honesty. It is so much easier to settle for muddling along, trying to keep everyone happy, doing what we have always done and are comfortable with, or just trying to survive. The problem is that a church taking that attitude is less likely to be around in ten years' time than one that seeks to develop its health.

In other words, death is certain! We will either die, and cease to function, because we were unwilling to address areas needing attention in the life of the church; or we will follow Christ as we die to some of the old patterns, habits and securities, and – in embracing healthier ways of operating – rise to a newness of life as a church about which we hardly dare dream.

Part of the costliness of bringing about change and growth in the life of the church is due to an important paradox in nurturing the health of a church. It is necessary to act both as if the health of a church cannot be developed without help from beyond the congregation and yet – at the same time – to act as though 'only we' can do anything about this situation. Both approaches are true but need to be held together. The next two sections address the two sides of this paradox.

'It's beyond us'

To acknowledge that we do not have or know all the answers is a healthy attitude in the whole of life. Those who think they do 'know it all' not only become bores but cease to learn from life. Indeed openness to God, others and the whole of life, was a mark of the life of Christ.

So it is good to look for resources from beyond ourselves. Ultimately this is expressed in prayer. It is also expressed in seeking to learn from others, listening to the stories of other churches, asking for help from others (such as a facilitator), and making use of the very considerable number of resources that are available today. Those resources have been made vastly more accessible by the internet.

The section on page 152, entitled, *Resources for healthy churches*, points not only to a range of resources but also to other lists of resources.

What that section cannot really do justice to is the fact that often the greatest resource is other people. Most Church of England dioceses have a range of sector ministers as well as churches that have much to give to help churches looking to develop their life. Equally, other denominations have specialist ministries on which one can draw. The secret is to ask around and to encourage as many members of the church as possible to keep their ears and eyes open to others who might be able to help us – even if simply by having a conversation with us.

For some the value of these resources is that someone has gone before us, addressed the issue we are concerned about and has developed (and almost certainly tested) materials which are now available to us. *Alpha* is a good example of that dynamic.

For others, the value of resources is that they get our thinking and action going and prompt us to rework what others have done in a way better suited to the particular context in which we are working.

Whether we are more at home adopting wholesale what others have done or adapting the work of others to our situation, the *Resources* list can be a valuable source of a great variety of approaches.

'We have it within us'

Wonderful though such resources can be it is also true that churches become healthy only in so far as they wrestle with questions they do not know the answer to, address issues that seem stubbornly to have resisted treatment in the past and dare to draw upon the resources of the present members of the church.

What we have to dare to believe is that God is able to equip *this group of people* with his grace to find the right answers and find the way through.

> One church was aware of its lack of a sense of purpose or direction and decided to seek to discover what God wanted of it. It took them eighteen months of study, prayer, discussion and exploration before they felt they were clear about being an *inclusive* church. Since then a whole range of groups of people, not usually seen in church, have found their way into the life of the church.

For some churches this is a painful course; daring to admit both that something is not right and also that – for the present – we simply do not know the answers. Daring to hold ourselves in that situation is what is most likely to open up the doors of creativity.

Every church, and the leadership in every church, is unique; which means simple solutions do not always work. There is a place for specific suggestions that may help to get things going but perhaps the most important thing to be said is that discerning our own situation and developing our own plans is what matters. Indeed there is so much to be gained from the process of developing our own plans, not that this rules out practical external resources. It is just that 'us designing what we are going to do' in an essential element in the journey to health for a church. As is the recognition of the particular gifts within any church and the willingness to draw on that most vital resource, one another.

> A church decided to start an additional Sunday service because young families were moving into the area and the

current services did not connect with them. The problem was they could not find an organist for the service. Instead of waiting to find one they managed to employ one short term, determined to draw on whatever musical gifts emerged out of this new congregation. Then a new family arrived and the man turned out to be someone who worked full-time as a saxophonist with an international orchestra. Within a year, the musical aspect of that congregation's worship was led by this man. There were thirty-six members of the congregational orchestra. Sixteen of them were children learning to play the recorder at school.

Working with what we have means that everyone can be involved and we can draw on the gifts of a great variety of people. We will quite probably discover all sorts of talents and abilities in the church that we never knew about. Furthermore, there is much less need to 'sell ideas' when people have themselves been involved in designing them and are involved in the unique local expression of them.

In the final issue it is a matter of local creativity: 'it is necessary for congregations to make their own discoveries when they try to understand what God is expecting of them today.'[3]

Chapter 7
Facilitating healthy churches

One of the major discoveries in developing the healthy churches material has been the value of a good external facilitator. This is true both for the initial event, doing the Church Profile Exercise, and for the long-term process of taking action to develop the health of the church. Indeed neither will happen unless they are properly facilitated, so any church engaging with this material needs to make decisions about how it is going to be facilitated. While this chapter focuses particularly on the use of an external facilitator, it applies just as much to churches that intend to use the material without such help.

There is certainly plenty to managing, as a cursory glance at Chapter 11 (*The Church Profile Exercise*) will show, so it helps to draw on the skills of someone who is familiar with the material and has had experience of handling it. The process really needs church leaders, and particularly clergy, to play a full part in the process. That is made much more difficult if they are also running the process.

There are other benefits that an external facilitator brings to the process. Objectivity is one. This is so not only in addressing weaknesses, but just as much in owning strengths. We all know that someone else telling us we are good at something is very affirming. Even if we thought we were good at that particular thing before being told so, it is still a great help to have it spoken out. Even more so is that the case when what others perceive as our strength and gifts are things we had not previously recognized. It is just the same with a church.

A further value of a good facilitator is that they can keep us up to the mark in working through the whole process. It is not untypical for a church to do the Church Profile Exercise but not to do anything about it after that event. Having a facilitator means that someone outside the situation has permission to ask what has been done and, if the answer is nothing, then to help the church return to the subject.

Facilitators can also be a good source of ideas when it comes to deciding what needs to be done. For example, a church may decide to work at *operating as a community*. Deciding to do so is the easy part. The difficult part is discerning *what we could do that would make a difference*. A good facilitator is likely to have ideas or will be in touch with networks through which they can find out ideas and possibilities.

Facilitators often have an important role in suggesting what might be dropped from the church's current programme. This is about giving practical expression to the seventh mark, namely, *doing a few things and doing them well.* Someone outside the situation can often see options more clearly here.

Establishing a relationship with a facilitator

A relationship between a church and a facilitator is like any relationship. It may be an enjoyable, but one-off, experience, or it may grow into something significant and long-lasting, or it may not work well. Three ways in which such relationships have been handled have emerged. They are as follows.

Sometimes a facilitator is asked to run a Church Profile Exercise. In other situations a facilitator is asked to run the Church Profile Exercise with an agreement to review any further involvement after the exercise. Further engagement would be on the basis of a rolling review in which either side is free to decide that the facilitator has completed what they can usefully do.

The third pattern has been to agree, from the start, for the facilitator to work with the church both to manage the Church Profile Exercise, and to stay with the church until discernible progress is evident in the implementing of action plans resulting from that process. Typically this actually involves running the Church Profile Exercise and then returning three times to a church council meeting every six months to spend an hour together reviewing progress and deciding further action needed. It has certainly proved valuable for churches to have a structure in which they can continue to review progress. Otherwise the vision that emerges at the beginning of the process gets lost in all the other demands that press for attention on the church's agenda.

These are three options for churches when deciding what use to make of a facilitator. They also describe three things that facilitators can offer. Some may not feel able to offer more than doing the Church Profile Exercise. It is important to offer what we can do. Nothing is gained by taking on what we cannot do.

Certainly, having an arrangement for long-term facilitation of the process, whether those arrangements are formal or informal, suggests that the church has grasped the fact that the reason for doing the Church Profile Exercise is in order to identify and implement long-term achievable actions that will develop the health of the church.

It is recommended that practical details, including such matters as travel expenses, are dealt with clearly and generously. Caring for facilitators who will work hard on our behalf really matters.

Finding a facilitator

There are two ways to go about finding someone suitable to act as facilitator for the healthy churches process.

Someone may have previously had some relationship with the church, and could be invited back. It is good to build on such relationships. Such a person may have some role in the wider church, such as an archdeacon or rural dean, or be a representative of a para-church organization. They may be part of another denomination or a member of a religious community.

It is worth remembering that church members may well, in their working life, have experience of doing facilitation work. They are likely to be helpful in deciding whom to invite. They might even do the job themselves, though there can be a loss of objectivity if an 'internal appointment' is made.

The other way to find a facilitator is to work through the official channels of the church. In the Church of England this would mean approaching sector ministers such as a diocesan missioner, parish development officer, adult education or lay training personnel. Alternatively, the archdeacon should be able to point a church in the direction of a suitable source of facilitators.

Other denominations have their own parallel roles, posts and structures. It is stimulating and creative to think ecumenically and to make contact with churches of other denominations who will have access to such people.

Another possibility is to approach para-church organizations, such as the Church Pastoral Aid Society, USPG and CMS field officers, Scripture Union, or the Bible Society (see *Resources* section for more details). There are also other people working freelance who are involved in the work of facilitation.

Where churches are doing the process as part of a wider grouping it is likely that facilitators will have been trained with this task specifically in mind, so that may be the obvious starting point. Where this is so, a helpful part of the training of facilitators will be in enabling them to sit in on a situation where someone else is facilitating. Seeing it done is usually the best way to learn what is involved.

Between them these various means should make it possible for any church to find a facilitator to help them in managing the process.

Preparing to facilitate

The healthy churches process is about helping a church to reflect on its life, before God, to discern the church's present experience of God's call on its life together, and to make progress in living out that vocation. Facilitation is, therefore, a spiritual discipline.

So *prayer* is the right and necessary starting point in the work of facilitation. This will involve prayer both for the church and for oneself. It is good, whenever possible, for facilitators to invite friends or some small group to pray for them through their engagement with a church, whilst respecting the confidentiality of this role. It is worth remembering that religious communities are usually delighted to support individual churches in prayer. They could be invited to pray for the church during the process. If so, they need to be kept informed about what is happening as the process progresses.

Prayer also needs to be made for the church. This will involve thanks-giving both for its readiness to engage in such a process and for the good things in its life already evident. It also includes thanksgiving for the people who will be involved in the process and for the varied gifting and insights they will bring to the work. Prayer needs also to be made that the group with which the facilitator will be working will be able to participate freely and creatively in the whole process.

Having a *right attitude* to this work is clearly vital. It is a spiritual discipline akin to being a spiritual director for a whole community. Ultimately, the task is to help the church *seek to find out what God wants*. It is about helping a church to express more of the life of Christ in the very way it operates. This is essentially a servant role; though often people end up wanting to treat their facilitator like a guru. The fact is that churches need to discern what God is calling them to be and do. The facilitator's role is to assist in the process of discernment.

Some *knowledge* of the church will also help. It is usually best to check out with the leadership of the church that they are happy for a facilitator to do the things suggested below, but some engagement with the leadership and the church community before managing the Church Profile Exercise is bound to enrich his or her understanding of the history and underlying dynamics at work in the life of the church.

Certainly, at the least, there needs to be a meeting with the minister/incumbent at which the nature of the commitment of the facilitator can be established. This is also an opportunity to begin to discover something of the history and present opportunities, issues and challenges facing the church – at least as seen from the perspective of this person's role in the church. If at all possible, some conversation with one or two church members is of great value in giving a lay perspective on the situation.

Attending a Sunday service is a valuable experience that says much about the evidence, or lack of evidence, of a number of the marks of a healthy church.

It may be appropriate to sit in on a church council prior to doing the exercise, or simply meeting with some group, such as a Mothers' Union, or home group, to get their perspective on the life of the church. Obviously such engagements need to be discussed and agreed with the church leadership first and are in any case dependent on the amount of time the facilitator is able to give to the whole process.

Facilitating the Church Profile Exercise

As far as the Church Profile Exercise is concerned there are three distinct parts to the work of facilitating that event.

Management of the exercise. This is a substantial piece of work. Preparing for that task is dealt with in Chapter 10 (*Preparing for the Church Profile Exercise*), and running it in Chapter 11 (*The Church Profile Exercise*). Because of the detailed nature of this work a good number of facilitators have drawn in another person to help with the practical management of the exercise. Such a person may be someone who is considering becoming a facilitator in due course. Equally they may simply see their role as being an 'administrative assistant' to the facilitator.

Introducing the marks of a healthy church. This is the heart of the Church Profile Exercise. Chapters 2, 3 and 4 are the source material for making this presentation. As it is best to keep that presentation to not more than five minutes per mark, the material from those chapters should be handled selectively, with one eye on the particular church with which one is working. Whilst illustrations can be drawn from the above chapters, it is always best to use personal stories where they are available.

Facilitating the process. This is about drawing out insights from people, stimulating conversation and with sensitivity to the underlying dynamics of the group. Helping people to listen to one another is all part of this work. It is a good idea for facilitators to develop a stock of questions they can draw on. That stock might include some of the following:

- Why do you think that is so?
- Where do you see that happening here?
- Can you give me some evidence of that?
- What do you think you/we could do about that?
- What would you like to see happening in the situation?

Questions that have a negative slant or imply criticism need to be avoided. The task is to open up minds and conversations. This is never achieved by putting people down.

Long-term facilitation

Beyond the running of the Church Profile Exercise itself, there is a task of facilitation in *keeping the process moving*. Churches easily become distracted by the sheer hard work of keeping everything going and addressing major pressing issues. Part of keeping the process moving may well be *offering suggestions* about what the church might consider doing. The facilitator also has an important role to play in the task of what is called 'resource investigation'. This is the technical term for finding people and programmes that may be of help. For example, a church may have decided that as part of its development of its *outward-looking focus* it wants to set up a meeting with representatives of the local community to help it understand, and establish partnerships with, the wider community. It would be a great help to hear from a church that has done just this or from someone who has facilitated such a process. The facilitator needs to ask around and this may well be wider than the denomination or the diocese. The *Resources for healthy churches* section gives a range of materials to help with each of the marks of a healthy church. It is an obvious starting point in looking for suitable resources.

A further part of the long-term work of facilitation is to help a church *work through emerging issues*. Sometimes that involves addressing conflicts, confronting power issues or dealing with long-buried pain from the past that is colouring the present life of the church. It may also simply be about the church's having set off with high hopes of developing some mark of a healthy church and finding that its efforts have been like water running into the sand.

The good news is that, because the gospel at its very heart is about life out of death, addressing these very issues can be the means of releasing much creative and visionary energy. It can be like taking a ball and chain off a prisoner's foot, for churches can all too easily find themselves imprisoned by the past.

Facilitators need to remember that, if they find themselves dealing with such matters as community conversations or managing conflict, they may need to recognize this is not their particular gifting and so need to suggest that someone else is brought in to help the church at this stage.

Arguably the most vital role of the facilitator who is working long term with a church is assisting in *nurturing the marks* in the church with which they are working. This is essentially about helping the church to practise the marks of a healthy church in the very act of engaging with the process. This may be the most important role the facilitator plays: helping the marks of a healthy church become part of the lifeblood of a PCC or other leadership group (see the 'transforming pilgrimage' section on pages 51–3). That would be a great gift to a church and a major contribution to its long-term health.

Guidelines for facilitators

So how can one do a good job of facilitation? Here are a number of pointers for those called to this demanding but often life-giving ministry in the life of a church.

Being an active listener. This is about reading the whole situation. It involves not only listening to the actual words spoken but to the underlying emotions with which they are said, to whom they are directed, and what they say about the dynamic of the group. Are contributions largely defensive or critical, or are they searching and open to new possibilities? What do such contributions tell us about 'who runs this place'? Listening, rightly understood, is one of the most challenging things we can do; just as being really listened to is one of the most precious gifts any of us can receive.

Active listening also involves reporting back to someone what we have heard them say. Particularly where someone may have been very emotional or rambled quite a bit it can help the discussions to say something like: 'Is what you are saying that . . .?' We need to say it in such a way that they can then correct our perception of what they have been saying.

Being encouraging. People will find it much easier to contribute if they feel the facilitator is listening and is aware of the emotions with which they are speaking. This sometimes involves protecting those who have made themselves vulnerable by saying something that the group may need to hear but finds difficult to accept. Encouraging and affirming all who contribute will help the group become open, not just to the facilitator but, more importantly, to each other. Drawing people out, encouraging them to speak their minds, is what the task is about. It is rather like being the conductor of an orchestra, only here one is conducting a conversation.

Never criticizing. Telling people off, especially in public, showing up someone's ignorance, or putting people down, are all destructive acts that take something away from a group's openness to facilitators and to each other. It will make people much less likely to reveal what they think, in case they get treated the same way.

Being sparing with good advice. The facilitator's role is not to tell a church what to do but rather to help the church discern and decide its own actions for itself. This does not rule out occasional advice born of experience, but facilitation is largely a non-directive task.

Being willing to ask hard questions. This is a vital, but tough, part of being a facilitator. It can help to remember that there will almost always be people who have been longing that someone would dare to ask that question and have never had the courage to do so, never felt they had the right words to use, or have actually been saying that but not been heard. Fulfilling this part of the task will serve them and the health of the church.

Attending to one's own feelings. There are times when a facilitator may feel criticized, or the lightning conductor of someone's anger of the church or leadership. Facilitators need to be able to recognize and deal with their own responses to what is going on and not to project their feelings onto the group and the process.

Summarizing. Facilitators can help the process keep moving forward by gathering up and restating the discussion so far. Without this focused contribution the discussion can go round and round.

Asking open-ended questions. 'How?' rather than 'What?' questions work best. If someone makes a claim or statement, for example about the strength or otherwise of one of the marks of healthy churches in this church, then something like 'can you illustrate that from your own experience?' is a helpful question. It is easier for an outsider to ask that question because the participants are then instructing the facilitator, but it does also help to draw out what people are talking about when otherwise they may just be generalizing.

Keeping the task in mind. Another important contribution a facilitator makes is to keep the group focused on the task. So keeping the task in mind is likely to involve reminding the group from time to time what the task is and bringing it back to focus on it.

Keeping a journal of one's facilitating work. This is one way of making sure that in helping others to reflect, learn and move forward, facilitators themselves are doing just that. The best time to do so is immediately after doing some facilitation work, when they still *feel* the experience. They should identify what they feel good about and what they reckon they achieved. They should note any major turning points, or road blocks, they were aware of and spot any ways in which, with hindsight, they could have handled the situation better. Any area in the work of facilitation where they feel more help is needed should be recorded. Then they should find someone with more experience to turn to for advice and practical suggestions.

The above points illustrate just how stretching, and fulfilling, the work of facilitation is. It can be life giving both for the group or church with which a facilitator is working and to facilitators themselves as they learn more about themselves, the church and how people work together. It will also continually remind them what the good news of Christ is all about and looks like as lived out in the lives of Christians seeking to serve God together.

Facilitator training

One of the most valuable resources for any facilitator is a person or group with whom they can engage whilst actually working through the process with a church. Our culture tends often, in training, to overload people with theory before they do something and under-support them while doing so. Yet most of us learn 'on the job' and from experience. The better pattern, therefore, is *a modest amount of training before* and a *good amount of support during* the work of being a facilitator.

When someone is working on their own, having been asked by a single church to act as its facilitator, then there may be limited opportunity to receive training. However, enquiring from sector ministers, and indeed from work situations where facilitators work, can uncover informal 'personal tutoring' that can be immensely helpful in giving someone the skills and confidence to take on the task. There are books that can help.[1]

Further help comes from working with someone else, whether they see themselves as a facilitator or not. Being able to talk over 'how things went' can be very instructive and supportive. The important thing is to build in time for debriefing as soon after each engagement with the group as possible, whilst impressions – and indeed, emotions – are still accessible. Encouragements, struggles and questions can be creatively addressed in this way.

Where groups of churches, such as a Churches Together group, deanery or diocese, are engaging in a healthy churches process then it is good to train, commend and deploy facilitators. Part of such work also involves establishing who has overall responsibility both for the training and for ongoing support of facilitators. This is a key role when groups of churches are working together on the healthy churches material.

Content of initial facilitator training

As far as initial training is concerned, usually something like a Saturday day (10a.m.–3.30p.m.) or an extended Saturday morning (9.30a.m.–12.30p.m.), or a couple of evening sessions, is sufficient. There are several things such a gathering could achieve. These include introducing potential facilitators to the following areas.

The Healthy Churches *material.* This is the necessary starting point. The best way to do this is to take them through the process as if they were a single church themselves. The profile may be rather more scattered in its scoring than most churches and thus be more difficult to work with. One way round this is to have one specific church's profile to hand and work with that.

To each other. This is particularly important if there are plans to work together in pairs. This can be done by getting people in groups of three or four to say something about themselves, how they came to be at this meeting, and what experience – if any – they have had in working as facilitators. Getting to know one another will also be happening as people work on the materials together and during the break times.

To good practices in facilitating. This would cover the sort of areas highlighted above under the heading *Guidelines for facilitators*, amplified and illustrated from personal experience and observation. This works best when there are also some small group exercises in such skills as active listening and the development of a list of open-ended questions that it is valuable to have to hand when working with a church. It is also good, particularly where there is an experienced facilitator to hand, to have a Question and Answer session. This can be the place where natural anxieties about what people are taking on can be brought out into the open and addressed.

To good endings. At some stage the relationship will need to come to an end. It is good to mark that in some way. It is also really good to help churches mark their progress through the whole process by simple acts of celebration. Parties and thank yous make the world a happier place and more like the kingdom.

The spiritual dimension. It is vital that this sort of training does model the marks of a healthy church, not least in being energized by faith and seeking to find out what God wants. Time for prayer together and for reflection on the experience really matters. It can also be really helpful to model possible ways for facilitators to enable a church group or PCC to pray together.

Part 3:
Seeing the
whole picture

Chapter 8
What is church?

Walking down the high street of a Yorkshire dales village, a friend and I passed a middle-aged man talking to a woman in her early thirties. After we had passed I said, 'did you notice the vicar?' Looking round, my friend said 'he looks a bit scruffy for a vicar, doesn't he?' Dressed for all the world as if he were a farmer, that was a valid point, except it was the *woman* who was the vicar. We had a good laugh at how our unconscious assumptions catch us out.

That is often what happens when engaging with the healthy churches material. Indeed, times when those of us involved in developing this material have had our unconscious assumptions uncovered have been noted earlier. One was when the original 25 churches proved not to be large churches in leafy suburbs but from a wider range of settings. Another example was when we found that these growing churches were typified not by being frantic, just running faster than other churches, but by *doing a few things and doing them well*. A further example was the discovery that these churches were not majoring on growing, but simply on doing a good job of being church.

Having our unconscious assumptions challenged has greatly assisted our understanding of how to work with churches to develop their health.

This process of challenging our unconscious assumptions is an important part of the healthy churches process. It evangelizes a church's understanding of what really matters and what is involved in developing the health of a church. It has proved to be one of the most valuable parts of the whole exercise for some churches.

Introducing 'mental models'

The term used to describe our unconscious assumptions is our 'mental model'. So, before we go any further, we would do well to try to get hold of our *unconscious mental model* of church. It is an important question because it so controls the assumptions and expectations about what church really is.

Archbishop Rowan Williams, when asked at a conference what his definition of church was, replied along the lines of: 'church is what happens when the impact of Christ on a situation brings two or more people together'. What is surprising about that definition is what it leaves out. There is no mention here of Word, sacrament, priest, building, public worship and much else besides. But it is a mental model that gets back to the heart of what church is all about. In times of change that is vital for us to do.

In an earlier book I gave a working definition of most people's mental model of church[1] (slightly reworked here) as being:

Church = Building + Priest + Sunday Services

That is what we recognize as 'church'. This mental model shapes not just our understanding of what church is but also how we then participate in its life. So 'keeping church going' is seen as keeping buildings open, finding the money to keep a priest (or at least part of one) and getting enough people into the building on a Sunday to keep the services going. That is what 'church work' – at its heart – is all about.

But is it? In times of major change and upheaval, such as the whole of our culture has been going through for several decades, everything can appear to be threatened. Our instinct is simply to defend what we value. A better way may be to go back to basics and ask the vital questions about what we are trying to do here. What may be needed is for us to adapt to the changes going on around us; but we cannot adapt 'it' unless we are clear what 'it' is. So we need to go back to first principles and think again about what church really is all about.

> A small congregation of a dozen members was forced to think again about church because, for different reasons, both the vicarage and the church had just been demolished. As they sat down and thought about the future they started to 'dream dreams' about 'what might be here in ten years' time'. They began this dreaming with great confidence, describing the new church building, with spire, and the choir stalls and robed choir, the churchwardens with the 'wands of office' and the Mothers' Union Enrolling Officer. Yet even as the ideas began to tumble out, they also began to slow up and become more hesitant. Then one member said: 'we are describing everything that has not worked for the last 20 years since we began as a church'. That led them to think about the church in a whole new way. They then changed tack and started to talk about what they could do to serve the local community, and how they could support each other in their faith. What emerged, and grew to over 60

within a decade, was something very different from their first ideas. It was hard work shifting out of their original mental model of church.

One way of approaching the task of nurturing the health of the church today is to address our unconscious mental model at this point. What we need is an understanding of church that gets to the heart of what it is all about. Here is one such way of developing a different approach to church that takes us back to what church is essentially about.

Church = community + faith + action

Church is essentially a *community* of people drawn together by *faith* in and encounter with Jesus Christ as Lord, which leads them to take *action* in the whole of life, living by a different set of values from what would otherwise have been the case. This living will involve a wide range of 'actions' including both *attitudes* (such as listening or generosity) and *actions* (service, confrontation or care). Sometimes the most important change a church can embrace is a change of attitude rather than any organizational change.

Another way of putting these three words (community, faith, action) is to describe the church as an *engaging faith community*. Engaging not just in the sense of being attractive, but rather, primarily, as involved with the world around us, following after the pattern of the Incarnation.

Good news for healthy churches

The power of mental models stems from their being unconscious. We do not realize that we are being shaped by them. Equally, once we pay attention to them and discover what they are, we can break free of their constraining influence.

An immediate value of uncovering our mental model of church is that it focuses thinking and action. The above working definition, of church as *an engaging faith community*, can immediately help any church to identify what it needs to work on. Indeed, in working with churches, especially where it is not possible to spend the amount of time needed to engage with the healthy churches process, it can be very productive to explore those three themes.

As far as *faith* goes, some of the questions that can uncover what is going on (or not going on) in this area are:

■　　What motivates those who are involved in the life of this church?

■　　Why do people come to this church? (Note: we so often ask why people do *not* come to church: it can be wonderfully enlightening to identify why they *do* come.)

■　　What does this church do to nurture the faith and faith development of church members?

■　　What do we do to help enquirers explore the faith?

■　　What is the effectiveness of what is done to nurture faith?

Undergirding these questions is a shift in the very nature of the Christian faith, which is taking place today. For centuries the faith has been given expression, primarily and most visibly, in the Church as an institution, classically in England in the established Church. Other forces now affect how Christianity is seen and engaged with. There is a continuing erosion of the Western Christendom background to our society. The individual has replaced the community as the natural starting point for considering almost any issue. Our society is moving beyond the scientific urge to analyse things to the more holistic interest in looking for points of integration and connectedness between the different aspects of a fragmented world and life.

All the above factors mean that Christianity needs to pay less attention to being a religious institution and more to providing *resources for living*. So the vital question to ask about any church is whether those who engage with it are finding resources that enable them to make sense of life, receive it as a gift, enjoy it and share in God's desire to spread goodness, generosity, welcome, justice and peace to all.

As far as *community* goes some of the key questions here are:

■　　How far does this church function as an organization that people are invited to *join* or as a community to which they can *belong* and make their contribution?

■　　Is this a place where people go to find somewhere to be honest, to share pain, joy, doubts and fears; or are we all too nice to dare to do anything like that?

■　　Is this a place where people can be real about themselves and discover their gifts, finding a sense of vocation and freedom to offer what they can rather than fit in with what is required?

■　　Is this a place where we do a good job of celebrating our joys and sharing our sorrows? Are laughter and tears welcomed or avoided?

In days when the church seems short of people, energy, money and resources, we can all too easily, and with the best of intentions, become a very driven organization fighting for survival.

> The priest in one church suffered from a serious illness that left him with very little energy to do anything. Indeed, taking the baptisms, weddings, funerals and Sunday services was the outside limit of what he could do. So things started to fall apart. Some in the church saw this and urged him to take early retirement. Understandably his response was 'I cannot afford to retire on a reduced pension'. Faced with this situation, a group of church members got together to decide 'what can we do?' Their Christian response was 'all we can do is to love our priest'. They sought to do so but the church continued to decline. Eventually he did reach retirement age, a new young priest was appointed and the church went from strength to strength. When asked why the church had grown, the church members said 'because we have a new priest'. The new priest gave a different perspective. 'This church', he said, 'is the church that forgot to stop loving the vicar.' In their struggle and Christian response to this situation community had been developed. Yes, the new priest was doing a good job of nurturing this community, but it had been brought into being before he came on the scene.

In a culture that is fragmented and highly mobile the church proclaims its good news by demonstrating the character of God as Trinity through being an open and welcoming community. That is our calling – to be good news as true community. As Moltmann has put it: 'God as love is experienced not in large organisations and institutions but in communities in which people can embrace each other.'[2]

As far as *engaging* is concerned, some of the questions likely to uncover the quality of engagement in a church are:

■ In what ways are we, as a church, involved in the local community?

■ How far do we do things *for* the wider community and how far do we do things *with* them?

■ What do we do to *listen* to the world around us?

■ How do we find out and draw upon the skills and gifts that church members bring from the whole of life?

■ How far does what happens in church help church members live out their faith in the whole of life, not just in what they do in church?

■   What do the sermons and intercessions in Sunday worship say about how the church sees its relationship with the world around?

The supreme model here is the life of Christ, the incarnate one. In the final issue, when God desired to communicate himself to the world, he did not just send a message, or even a messenger. He came himself.

Mental models often surface at this point. When churches are asked 'how involved are you in the local community?' the answer is almost invariably an organizational one about the vicar being a school governor and our running a club for the elderly. These are fine as far as they go, but the greater engagement is with church members living out their lives. As Robin Greenwood has put it: 'For the vast majority of laity . . . the main focus of their ministry lies in the opportunities presented by their everyday responsibilities.'[3]

> **A church was looking for a new vicar. A small inner core of 'keen church workers' drew up a job description. Essentially this was about the task of getting more people from the fringe of church into the centre. When the new vicar arrived he made a disturbing discovery. These 'fringe' people were not loosely connected with the Christian faith. They were as committed to following Christ as 'the core': but they were expressing it through their work, local community and leisure involvement. So the vicar, as he put it, 'joined the fringe', working to help people live out their faith in the whole of life. The church flourished, but the vicar got into a lot of trouble and received much hostility from the original 'core' for betraying his 'calling'. It was a costly path that he chose.**

A 'mixed economy' church

In days of profound change it is important to get to the heart of an issue. Too easily, when the church's life is threatened not least by lack of resources, we lapse in to the familiar and seek to keep 'church as we know it' going. Yet the very challenges actually open a door to fresh exploration.

We can do that by going back to first principles and asking *what are we trying to do here?* It is particularly good to do this when there seem to be strong and unproductive arguments. It can be a wonderful way to find a new path on which to venture. It raises questions that may well get us in touch with our deepest faith, our sense of vocation and our understanding of what life and church are all about. Energizing faith can often burst to the surface by this means. This may well lead a church to consider a different way in which to operate and *be* church.

Inherited and emerging modes of church

Here it is helpful to have, as part of a healthy mental model, an understanding of two major ways in which the life of the church is finding expression today. One can be called *inherited mode*. This is about church as we know it, where buildings, priests and Sunday services play central roles. It can be of great help to the church in this situation to remember that our primary calling is to be an engaging faith community.

But the church today is also finding different ways of expressing its life. Various terms are currently in use to describe these new developments. They include 'new ways of being church', 'church planting', 'cell church', 'Minster church', 'small faith communities', etc. This takes us into the realm of the *emerging mode* of being church. Some have objected to this term as essentially too passive. All we can do, they would point out, about something that is 'emerging' is sit around waiting for it to emerge. Clearly we need to be more proactive.

However, the term points to something important, namely that these new ways of being church often happen spontaneously. Indeed, those involved in these fresh expressions of the life of the church may be the last people to recognize that what is taking place here is 'church'. So a vital part of our work is to keep our eyes and ears open for what, by the action of the Holy Spirit, is coming to life around us.

The other task is to avoid any sense of competition between church in *inherited* and *emerging* modes. There is so much they can learn and gain from each other.

> A Christian couple became involved in helping a drug addict to break their addiction. After a long struggle the addict broke free and, furthermore, caught the faith of the couple. Soon afterwards the former addict introduced another addict to this couple. They too came to faith and found freedom from their addiction. In due course a group of over 50 was meeting together in a wonderful engaging faith community. When asked what nourished their faith they gave the surprising answer that it was sitting quietly in (preferably empty) church buildings and going to sung Eucharist at the nearby cathedral.

In the above story it was church in inherited mode that produced the couple in the first place and was now playing its part in nurturing the faith of this new faith community. And that new expression of church valued the old forms but also had some important things to teach church in inherited mode. In short, we need each other.

This raises important questions about the relationship between church as 'building + priest + Sunday services' to church as an *engaging faith community*. The goal is not to abandon buildings, priests and public acts of worship, but rather to harness these valuable resources to the higher and more fundamental goal of building churches that are *engaging faith communities*.

That is more likely to happen as we allow both our heritage of faith and the challenges of current circumstances to evangelize our mental model in such a way that we become open to new possibilities in the 'old' and in the 'new'.

Engaging with the healthy churches material is more than likely to raise these deeper questions about what is church, which may affect, profoundly and for the better, our understanding of 'what we are trying to do here'. We need to be alive and alert to that challenge, willing to venture into unfamiliar territory in response to it, and ready to improvise in ways that surprise and delight and yet ring true with the past, as we focus our vision on seeking to develop a variety of ways of being *an engaging faith community*.

Chapter 9
The angel of the church

There is a delightful story about Moses in Exodus.[1] He has been told to go to Pharaoh with the potentially life-threatening demand to 'let my people go'. Not surprisingly Moses asks for a sign, some reassurance that God would be with him. God says to Moses 'what is that in your hand?' That does not sound like a difficult question and Moses replies that it is his staff. He is told to throw it to the ground, whereupon it turns into a snake. He is then told to pick it up and it turns back into a staff. He is then, as a further sign, told to put his hand into his cloak. When he does so it becomes leprous and, when he repeats the action, it returns to its former healthy state. The key phrase in all this is 'what is that in your hand?' God chose to help Moses find the courage for the task ahead through things, literally, well within his grasp.

That is the experience of many churches seeking to develop their health. There are circumstances, not always comfortable ones, that immediately face them. In addressing them they find themselves giving expression to the marks of a healthy church. There are also gifts, skills, insights and experiences within the faith community that are the basic ingredients needed for the next stage of their faith journey.

This dynamic of finding the answers in taking hold of what is 'to hand' has been true also of the development of this material. Having established the seven marks and begun to work with them, deeper questions about the nature of church and the unconscious assumptions of what it is all about, as explored in the last chapter, started to surface. This raised the question of how to help churches engage with these deeper questions. Part, at least, of the answer lay in what Dr Janet Hodgson and I had 'in our hand'. For myself, the answer was 'a couple of books'. For Janet Hodgson it was a multitude of images. The story is as follows.

Whilst working with Janet Hodgson I had, at the same time, been reading a formative book by James Hopewell, entitled simply *Congregation*.[2] Soon after that, I began reading the equally striking and original trilogy on the Powers by Walter Wink.[3] I had also been reading about the shift in the business world from a focus on 'mission statements' to identifying the 'spirituality' of the organization. These various strands had made me aware of this very different, essentially holistic, way of looking at a church. It involves seeing church as a whole 'system' and entity, with its own ethos, culture and personality.

Janet Hodgson meanwhile had been doing work for a number of years with images of Christ, having been one of the pioneers of this approach in the UK. Among her extensive collection of several thousand such images were several hundred images of angels. It quickly became clear that this would be a helpful balance to the Church Profile Exercise. Collecting further images of angels, amassing (if that is the right term) well over one thousand such images, we began to explore their use in healthy church events.

It has proved a most valuable complement to the Church Profile Exercise. Over the years we have found that many people find this use of the imagination a great help in reflecting on the life of their church. It has opened doors that the analytical approach had not managed to do. It has also proved to be great fun as well as instructive.

Since then, almost invariably when addressing the subject of healthy churches, we have sought to use both the Church Profile Exercise and the approach outlined in this chapter about *the angel of the church*. A way to work with churches to identify their 'angel' is set out in Chapter 12 (*Angel of the Church Exercises*).

What we have found to work best is keeping together, in different ways, these two approaches of the Church Profile Exercise and the exploration of the *angel of the church* to which we now turn.

The angel of the church

The phrase 'the angel of the church' comes from chapters 2 and 3 of the book of Revelation. In chapter 1 there has been a description of John's vision of the risen Christ. There then come seven letters to seven churches in the area. The letter to the first church reads as follows:[4]

> *'To the angel of the church in Ephesus write: These are the words of him who holds the seven stars in his right hand, who walks among the seven golden lampstands:*
>
> *'I know your works, your toil and your patient endurance. I know that you cannot tolerate evildoers; you have tested those who claim to be apostles but are not, and have found them to be false. I also know that you are enduring patiently and bearing up for the sake of my name, and that you have not grown weary. But I have this against you, that you have abandoned the love you had at first. Remember then from what you have fallen; repent, and do the works*

*you did at first. If not, I will come to you and remove your
lampstand from its place, unless you repent. Yet this is to
your credit: you hate the works of the Nicolaitans, which
I also hate. Let anyone who has an ear listen to what the
Spirit is saying to the churches. To everyone who conquers,
I will give permission to eat from the tree of life that is in
the paradise of God.'*

The structure of each letter is the same. It can be seen in this first letter,
as follows.

- **The greeting:** from the risen Christ picks up an aspect of the vision
  of John, in this case about the seven stars and golden lampstands.
- **The address:** commending the church for the good things in its life
  and witness.
- **The challenge:** identifying where there is a lack of conformity to
  God's purposes and pointing to action that is needed.
- **The promise:** always addressed to 'those who overcome' and
  promising them some aspect of the revelation that is about to
  follow in the rest of the book: in this case 'permission to eat
  from the tree of life': overturning the command to Adam and Eve
  in the Garden.

The intriguing thing as far as we are concerned here is that each letter is
addressed to 'The angel of the church in . . .' The phrase sounds so foreign
to our modern ears that we do one of several things that can be seen in
the response of Commentaries on Revelation. Some are frankly so puzzled
that they make no comment and move straight into the text. We do the
same. What matters, we instinctively feel, is what the letter says, not to
whom it is addressed, especially if that address is obscure.

Others attempt to explore what the phrase might mean but most of these
are ways of explaining away the strangeness of 'the angel of the church'.
Some say it means the leader of the church; yet there are perfectly good
and much more easily understood words, such as elder/bishop. So why
use such a puzzling term? Others take the word 'angel' to mean that this
is the Guardian Angel of the church. Attractive though that idea sounds, for
it does take the use of the word 'angel' seriously, it does not fit the text.

What the text reveals, on closer inspection, is lost to our modern ears for
one particular reason. Modern English does not distinguish between the
singular and plural use of the word 'you'. So we miss the 'you singular'
of verses 2-7.[5] Once we grasp this we can see that the angel is being
addressed personally. It is *the angel* of the church in Ephesus that has

endured yet has lost its first love and needs to repent. So the 'angel' is the 'church', which is being addressed personally. The risen Christ is addressing the corporate identity of the church. The church is being seen as having a corporate personality.

The Chief Education Officer of a large city was being interviewed about some educational changes the Government of the day was making. In the midst of this interview the CEO was asked, somewhat out of the blue, 'so what makes for a good school?'(he could equally well have been asked about what makes for a *healthy* school). Without hesitation he answered: 'Oh, a good school is a school with a good spirit.' Nothing here about the state of the buildings, the community context or how high up the league table of examination results it had climbed. Here was the feel of the place and its effect on those involved in it. What he was describing was the essence of the school as a whole: its corporate identity.

So too, the angel of the church is about seeing churches as a whole and being able to discern their character, spirit, personality and feel. Walter Wink puts this concisely when he says: 'The angel of the church is the coincidence of what the church is – its personality – and what it is called to become – its vocation.'[6] That has proved a wonderfully helpful definition to work with.

Addressing church culture

Strange though this term 'angel of the church' may be, it actually expresses a way of seeing the church that is quite normal. We talk about church in terms of personality. 'That is a really depressed church.' 'That church has come alive recently.' 'That is a church that always seems to be chasing its tail.' 'You can never get any sense out of that church.' 'That church is so generous-hearted . . .' In such ways we talk about the church in terms of a single, corporate identity.

Another way in which we see church like this is the practice in some denominations of calling churches by the names of saints. It expresses this sense of churches having a personality or corporate identity.

Walter Wink links both present *personality* and *vocation* for the future. People are like that too. We are the interplay of who we are, our present personality, and the direction we are taking in life or our sense of vocation. That holds true even if we have no sense of direction. It is reflected in who we are and how we approach life.

Working with this understanding of the angel of the church helps us to get a different handle on the church and to understand its, often strange, inner dynamics. A self-righteous church, a fearful church, or a bruised church, each needs a quite different approach, even if their size, tradition and setting are the same.

Having reflected further on Walter Wink's description of the angel of the church and done further work with churches seeking to identify their angel, I would now want to amplify his definition by describing the angel of a church as the *interweaving of* . . .

- where the church has come from – its *history*
- where it is – its *context*
- what it is – its *personality*
- what it is called to become – its *vocation.*

Why does it matter?

The art of marriage has been described as like learning to play an instrument. We all know how to rub someone up 'the wrong way', provoking a negative response from them. In marriage the art is to bring the best out of another person. We grow into that in so far as we learn to 'read' the other. The same is true with churches. If we 'threaten' a 'fearful' church it will run and hide. What it needs is affirmation and encouragement. On the other hand, it may well be right to be much more direct and challenging to an 'arrogant church'. A complacent one needs yet another approach, which is why seeking to identify, at least in some measure, the angel of the church is such a valuable thing to do.

The more fully we can understand the personality of an individual, or a group, the more likely we are to be able to know how to help them to change and address new realities. Too easily we think that changing the structures is what will make a difference, yet – at best – such changes alter little, for the whole spirit, feel, ethos (in short, the angel) remains untouched. It is one of the ways in which the church betrays its mental model as being an organization rather than a community. Walter Wink says, rather, that 'real change must therefore affect not just the visible forms an institution takes, but somehow must alter the spirit, the core essence, of the entity as a whole'.[7]

The nature of the angel of a church

There are two particular things we need to know about the nature of an angel of a church if we are to make the best use of this way of developing the health of a church.

The first is that *the angel of a church is morally mixed*. It contains both good and bad. This is so despite our 'mental model' of angels that tells us that they are the embodiment only of the good. Think back to the angel of the church in Ephesus. The risen Christ commends the angel for 'your works, your toil and your patient endurance'. But he also speaks plainly about things that are not right: 'But I have this against you, that you have abandoned the love you had at first. Remember then from what you have fallen; repent, and do the works you did at first.'[8] In fact, the church in Philadelphia has no faults identified by the risen Christ and the church of Laodicea has no positive attributes named by Christ. More typical are the other five churches, which had strengths to affirm and failures that needed to be addressed and repented of. So we are likely to find that the angel of most churches is a mixture of strengths and weakness, good and bad. Again, just like us as individuals.

Second, *the angel of a church is essentially passive*. It is not the angel that changes the church. Rather, change happens the other way round. Choices and moral actions by the church on earth are what result in changes in the angel, which means that our task is not to pray to or at the angel of the church. For example, a church might have a 'poverty mentality' and so only give to charitable and missionary endeavours at the end of the year 'if there is anything left'. It might be that a visiting missionary challenges them about living generously and daring to give monthly. They start to do this, find they can do it and decide in the light of this positive experience to increase the amount the following year. The angel of that church is changing from 'tight-fisted' to 'open-hearted', *as a result of hard choices by the church*.

This should not really surprise us since we know how people change as a result of how they respond to their experiences in life. Someone may fail at something and as a result determine that they will conquer this matter, whilst another person retreats and avoids taking any risks again. The same circumstances, yet the different responses both reflect and affect the very character of the person. So too with the church.

However, before we think about changing the angel of the church we need first to consider how we can identify or name the angel of a church.

Naming the angel of a church

It takes time to be able to describe/name the angel of a church, as it takes time to understand and describe the personality of someone we know well. Moreover, it needs constant revision and updating. At best it involves the insights of *many people* to identify the angel of a church, since what is being described is itself a community of people. Though such discernment needs *individuals* to do their own work, a group will develop a richer picture than any one person can.

> An area bishop recently said, almost as a passing comment, 'the church in this area is reactive, going under and full of victim language'. He had been discerning the angel of the church in that area.

> A leadership team in one church thought about their church and identified the church as essentially *confident*, *diverse* and *frantic*.

A fine example, from the 'secular' context is provided by The Revd Angela Tilby,[9] (who formerly worked for the BBC), in the following extract from an address she gave.

> *I first read Walter Wink's material in the year when the BBC decided to relocate its religious programme-making department from London to Manchester. I found myself meeting a corporate ethos history which was new to me ... By the time I left the BBC I felt I knew the angel of BBC North rather well. I knew it was a friendly but prickly angel, anxious to be liked, defensive, vain; envious of others, a bit of a loud mouth and a bully, but kind and considerate if treated with respect ... When I left the BBC it was with a sense that attempting to discern the nature of the angel was a spiritually useful thing to do. Not only because it helps us locate ourselves within it, but because it helps us to discover what our mission is to the institutions and places we are sent to. Angels, remember, are appointed by God. They are part of the created reality of the life of nations and institutions. They hold God's call. They guard and subvert vocations.*

Working with the angel of a church

The primary purpose in considering the angel of a church is to discover how that angel can grow to greater health – measured by likeness to Jesus Christ. Working with the angel of a church involves *affirming the positives and addressing the negatives*, as happens in the seven letters to the churches in Revelation. It is about helping to mature the 'personality' of the church so it becomes a richer reflection of Christ. Working like this enables us to be in touch with something more profound and important than results from treating the church simply as an organization.

Some of the steps that have emerged in the work that has been done in this area are as follows.

Identifying the angel of the church

Clearly the starting point needs to be discerning the angel of the church. Though this is the obvious starting point it is work that is never complete, for the angel is always changing in response to what is happening in the life of the church. However, beginning this work is vital if we are to bring about real change in the life of a church. Churches benefit from developing a continual process of reflecting on the angel of their church.

Chapter 12 (*Angel of the Church Exercises*) offers several ideas of how to set about identifying the angel of a church. Once we have some understanding of the identity of the angel of the church, the next task is to find out how to work with that angel.

Addressing the angel of the church

Only when we have some understanding of who a person is and where, as we put it, 'they are coming from' can we begin to engage in real conversation with them. So, when we meet people for the first time we often ask lots of questions. Only when we have some awareness of who we are addressing can we 'speak our mind'.

> Addressing racism in America, Martin Luther King recognized it was more important to change attitudes than laws. So he spoke to what he called the 'soul of America'. Rather than getting into black/white confrontation, he spoke about America as 'the land of the free'. But not all, he pointed out, were free and this was the next step for them in being true to their destiny as a nation. Another line he took was to speak about America being a nation called to break new frontiers. He then pointed out that, although they had reached the western seaboard, this was not the 'last frontier'. Now there was a frontier of racial segregation that had to be broken through.

Addressing the angel of the church requires a similar understanding and imaginative approach. A fearful church needs to be helped to face, address and overcome those fears. A complacent church needs to get involved with pain, injustice, suffering, etc. A frantic church needs to be led into experiences of silence, stillness and to engage with what Vanstone has called 'the stature of waiting'.[10]

Taking the church through learning experiences

However many driving manuals a non-driver may read and however much they may know about the inner workings of the combustion engine, they will never become skilled in driving a car without getting into one and doing so. We learn most effectively by doing, by having a go. Looking, therefore, for appropriate 'learning experiences' is an important part of working with the angel of a church.

> A church building, built as a chantry chapel, had a sense of 'death' that affected not just the feel of the building but the culture of the church. The vicar arranged for a special All Souls' Requiem for the departed. The difference was noted by many and the 'dead hand of the past' significantly reduced.
>
> A small rural church, hesitant about its faith, linked up with a group going to Taizé and found its life transformed as a result of that striking experience, which bore little relationship to how churches normally function.

Major building projects often have an exodus-like impact on a church, leading them to experience many of the marks of a healthy church simply as a result of facing the challenges of such a project.

Discerning church 'vocation'

Walter Wink makes a fundamental distinction between the present personality of a church and what it is called to become. All that has been said so far is about seeking to identify this 'present personality'. The other side of the definition is equally important, especially when we put the two together.

The source of that vocation in the Revelation letters is the risen Christ. It comes in a number of ways. Partly it comes from the vision of the risen Christ recorded in the first chapter, since each church is addressed by some aspect of that vision. Our faith heritage is part of our present vocation.

Another element is the challenge embedded in each letter and noted in the framework of each letter above. So easily we miss this dynamic and imagine that vision is about our developing a programme and strategy. Vision is more about hearing what the risen Christ is saying to us – hence the importance of seeking to find out what God wants. The vocation is also embedded in the last part of each letter. Here churches are promised a share in what God is about to do in the whole of the created order. So too today. Vocation is about what God is doing in his world. We discover it when we 'stop starting with the church' and turn our attention to his loving purposes in the whole of life and the world around us. It will necessarily be a stretching vocation to share in his purpose of 'bringing all things to a good End'.[11]

This connects with the contemporary understanding of mission as essentially God's. Our, derived, mission is to join in with what God is doing. So, a church's vocation arises particularly out of the first three marks of a healthy church, namely:

■   Our faith encounter with Christ: that energizing faith that is the foundation of every healthy church.

■   Our engagement with the world around us: which takes us beyond church (and out of starting with the church to starting with God's world) into an outward-looking focus.

■   Our seeking to find out what God wants: not least through prayer, engagement with the Scriptures, our heritage of faith and our corporate ability to reflect on what God is saying to us in our present setting.

This gives a fresh approach to agenda setting in the life of the local church. In the era particularly of 'mission audits' very extensive, often predominantly statistical, research would be done to find out the needs of the community. Out of that an agenda would be developed. These agendas suffered from the twin demotivating factors of giving churches an impossibly large task whilst failing to connect it to any source of energizing that would be needed to take on such tasks.

More recently, the development of things such as Mission Statements or Mission Action Plans can suffer from being simply descriptions of what the church is already doing or a wish list of what we would like to see. Unless creatively handled they can all too easily involve a minimal amount of seeking to find out what God wants.

The real task is to engage with a church's sense of vocation, with the particular gifts of individual members of the church and with the faith that – rightly – should be the source of energy for what is done. Doing so will sharpen a church's focus, leading it to do a few things and do them well. That is definitely better than being submerged under an unattainable agenda.

Next steps

Working with the angel of the church can help a church make achievable progress in the following ways.

First, once we have identified the church's present personality and its vocation, it then becomes possible to see what the journey from one to another will involve.

> One church chose an angel hiding behind the playing of a large musical instrument as its angel of present personality. The angel was touched with reds and golds. They saw the church as focused around worship and (linking with the colours) experiencing something of the grace of God. Yet they recognized also that they were hiding behind excellence in worship and not coming out into the open in the community around them or about their faith.
>
> The angel of vocation was an earthy angel in the guise of a contemporary housewife. Through it they saw their calling as to be much more down-to-earth, connecting faith with daily living. The first step on this journey that they noted was the need to be honest about doubts, fears, disagreements and struggles rather than think that faith was best expressed by saying that 'everything in the garden is lovely' when everyone knew it was not.
>
> They had begun that journey into vocation and into greater health.

Second, the word angel means literally 'messenger'. As such the angel is the one who bears, carries, brings to birth, and then nurtures God's call to his Church, for the Church's vocation is a message about God's loving engagement with his world. Discerning the angel of vocation has the effect, then, of drawing together the spirituality of the church and its practical planning, so that the church lives out its calling from God.

When this happens the church increasingly embodies the good news. It becomes a living demonstration of what it believes and wants to share with others: an engaging faith community.

Part 4:
Healthy churches exercises

Chapter 10
Preparing for the Church Profile Exercise

Contained in this chapter are the following elements.

An *overview* of the five steps in the Church Profile Exercise.

A section on *preparing* for conducting the Church Profile Exercise.

A description of *different ways* in which the Church Profile Exercise has been run.

An outline of the *varied applications* of the *Healthy Churches* material.

Some thoughts on the spirit in which the exercise is done.

A *study guide* to the seven marks, suitable for use by study groups, as a basis for a sermon series or for use as the basis of meditation.

Figure 1 (on p. 106) gives a visual overview of the whole healthy churches process.

Church Profile Exercise: an overview

The exercise is designed to:

introduce people to the seven marks of a healthy church as set out in Chapters 2, 3 and 4;

help them *reflect* on the health of their church in the light of those marks;

and then *identify actions* best designed to develop the health of their church.

The Church Profile Exercise focuses on the first two parts of the above purposes and concludes with an initial exploration of possible actions. Preparing to run this exercise is the subject of this chapter.

There are five steps that constitute the Church Profile Exercise, which can be summarized in the following way.

Step one: introducing the seven marks

This involves someone giving a brief (not usually more than five minutes per mark) introduction to each of the seven marks. During the course of this introduction, or at the end, each person present is then asked to score the church on a scale of 1 (low) to 6 (high).

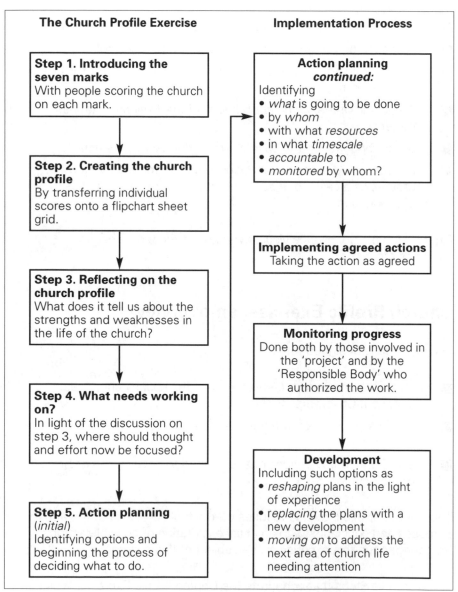

Figure 1: Overview of the whole process

Step two: creating the church profile

Individual scores are collected in and transferred to a large (flipchart-sized) grid so that a profile of the church can be seen.

Step three: reflecting on the church profile

The *church profile* is a visual representation of how the life of the church is seen by the participants of the exercise as measured against the seven marks of a healthy church. With that in front of them the group reflect on what that tells them about the life of their church. This is usually done by exploring three questions:

- What are our strengths?
- Where there is a wide divergence of scores, what is this saying?
- What is holding us back and needs to be addressed?

Step four: what needs working on?

In the light of the discussion at the previous stage an exercise now follows that helps the group identify specific areas for action. This is done by use of Action Lists filled in by participants. They are asked to identify one or two of the bullet points from the Summary Sheet that need attention. If none of the bullet points expresses what they see as needing attention, they are asked to put the issue in their own words.

Step five: action planning

This is only possible in an initial and exploratory way during the exercise itself. Most of what needs to be done will require time being allocated on the appropriate leadership group's agenda not long after the exercise has been done. This marks the start of the *implementation phase*.

The implementation phase will involve a number of elements, such as:

- agreeing the area(s) that needs addressing;
- generating a range of options to consider as possible actions;
- selecting the most appropriate next step (best if it is 'one step at a time');
- drawing up detailed plans for implementing agreed action(s);
- monitoring progress;
- celebrating progress to date;
- continuing with existing actions, revising or replacing them, as appropriate;
- moving on to the next area requiring attention and action.

One observation that has emerged as a result of using this material is that healthy churches are ones that are able to pay sustained attention to an issue and keep going, even when they meet obstacles. Unhealthy churches tend to have a short attention span and, if something does not immediately solve most of their problems, they tire and move on to something else. The result is that they neither benefit from plans that work nor learn from plans that do not produce the desired results. They lose out both ways.

Once a church has seen its initial plans through, it could usefully repeat the exercise, identify a new area for work and attention and repeat the process several times over the course of a sustained period of years.

Although some pointers are given in this chapter about the *implementation phase*, the main focus is on the running of a Church Profile Exercise. Help with managing the *implementation phase* is covered in Part 2 of the Handbook (*Growing healthy churches*) and especially in Chapter 6, *Developing healthy churches*.

Preparing to conduct the exercise

Timing of the exercise

The timings given for the whole process are built around *three one-hour sessions*, whether done at one meeting or a series of meetings. Although the timings can be reduced, there is a price to be paid for such abbreviation. Essentially, what is most likely to be restricted is the reflection and discussion time, which is the most crucial and creative part.

However, a variety of ways has been found of adapting this schedule to local needs. These other options are set out in the section on a shortened version (page 132) and the section on varied uses made of this material (page 113). Wherever possible, a good amount of time for the work means that unhurried and creative discussion is most likely to result.

When more than one meeting is planned, it works best if they are not more than a week or so apart. Doing the exercise in two meetings does create a difficulty arising from the fact that membership of the group is likely to change. This results in the need to explain what has gone before to those who were not at the prior meeting(s).

Identify the church group

■ *At least five people* from a church are needed for the exercise to work. Where a smaller number of people are involved it is best to tackle the whole process as a conversation rather than an exercise, keeping pieces of paper to a minimum. *It really works best with a group of between10 and 25 people.*

■ *Multi-parish benefices* need to decide whether to work as a benefice or as individual churches, or some combination of the two. There is no one right way.

■ *Larger churches* (150+) sometimes find it more fruitful to do the exercise with each of their main congregations.

With whom to do the exercise

■ Typically with a *church council* or *leadership group.*

■ Some churches have done it with *whole church meetings.* The largest single church group to date was over 120 people. It worked well, but how to transfer scores to a flipchart (or probably better, an overhead projector acetate) needs careful pre-planning.

■ Some have also worked with *a sample group* of older/younger/newer members. This has often been done as a 'control group' alongside a church council or leadership group. Where this is done it is best for the church council or leadership group to do the whole exercise first before looking at the scores from the other group. It should also be noted that, where there is divergence between the church council and the control group, this does not, of itself, say who is seeing the church more accurately.

■ Some have worked with the *regular congregation.* In this case it has often been linked to a preaching series on the seven marks. Each person present is given a card on which to score the church on the mark that has just been preached about. Here, care needs to be taken to ensure that the number of scores for each mark is the same, as clearly a larger congregation one week will seem to score that mark more highly. Percentages are the simplest way to deal with this, putting one tick for each ten per cent, so if 60 per cent of the congregation scored a mark '3', then six ticks would be put in that box.

■ Some churches have used a *combination* of the above.

Equip the meeting place

■ choose a *well heated/ventilated* room;

■ *moveable chairs* rather than fixed seating are essential;

- *enough space* is needed for people to circulate and form small groups;
- *a flipchart*, with plenty of pens and paper;
- *the list of seven marks*, on a flipchart-sized paper, as per Figure 2a, below.
- *Scoring Guide* (Appendix 2) on acetate or flipchart;
- *OHP and screen* if being used;
- Arrange details of *refreshments* for participants.

Mark	1 low	2	3	4	5	6 high	Total
1. Energized by faith							
2. Outward-looking focus							
3. Seeks to find out what God wants							
4. Faces the cost of change and growth							
5. Operates as a community							
6. Makes room for all							
7. Does a few things and does them well							

Figure 2a: Church Profile Sheet

Handouts – enough for everyone taking part (listed in the order in which they are used)

- *Church Scores Sheet* (Appendix 1)
- *The Seven Marks Summary Sheet* (Appendix 4)
- *Action Lists* (Appendix 5).

It is best not to hand out these papers at the start but as indicated in the text.

Helpers

The exercise (particularly with a group of 20 or less) can be facilitated by one person. However, there are considerable advantages in drawing on the help of others, not least in dealing with the practical arrangements, even when the group is below 20. Three or so is a suitable number unless the group is really large and needs more resourcing. Help should include managing practical matters such as setting out the room and providing drinks as people arrive and at various intervals during the exercise.

■ **creating the** *Church Profile Sheet:* with one person putting ticks onto the *Church Profile Sheet* (see Figure 2b, p. 124) and the others reading out the 'scores' from the *Church Scores Sheets* that have been collected in. So, if there are three people helping in the process, each can take a third of the sheets and call out the ticks against each mark in turn. All can also help add up and fill in the *Total* column on the *Church Profile Sheet* (see pp. 125–6 for details).

■ **creating the** *What needs working on* lists: the task is to make a separate flipchart-sized sheet for each mark listing the Action points suggested. Share sheets out between helpers. Make sure they write the mark at the top of the sheet, then list any points people have made.

Different ways in which the Church Profile Exercise has been run

Setting out the material here and in the following chapter is not intended to suggest that this is the only way of using this material. However, it is as well to bear in mind that it has been developed as a result of considerable use and road testing. Most of it is simply the fruit of what has found to be most effective.

So now, some of the patterns.

The standard framework

Typically this is done on a Saturday (or, less frequently on a Sunday) running either from something like 10.30a.m. to 3.30p.m. (with breaks for coffee and a shared lunch) or within a morning, working from around 9.30a.m. to 1p.m., allowing for at least one coffee break in the middle during which the profile is developed (step two).

The two-session approach

Typically this involves two evening sessions (one or two weeks apart). The first part can either be a straight one hour, which takes the church to the point where the church profile can be created (in the time before the next meeting). This then means that the second session needs to be longer (as near two hours as possible).

Alternatively, the first session can include introducing the marks, creating the church profile and an initial reflecting on the profile (steps one to three). The second session can pick up where the reflecting left off and then continue through to the end of the whole exercise. This alternative approach has the advantage of creating two sessions of equal length.

Sermon series context approach

Some churches have introduced the marks through a sermon series; either preaching on one mark at a time, or dealing with two at any one time rather along the lines of Chapters 2 to 4. Usually, when this is done, the congregation is given a form of the *Church Scores Sheet* to complete and hand in for the marks preached on at that service. By the end of the series much of the congregation will have been involved in scoring many of the marks. However, it does need to be borne in mind that numbers will not be the same and this needs to be allowed for in developing the *church profile*. Using percentages is often the easiest way of dealing with unequal numbers of people scoring different marks.

Having completed steps one and two in this way then makes it possible to deal with the rest of the process in a two-hour meeting. However, it is worth considering doing so in two ninety-minute sessions: the first one tackling steps three and four and the second session addressing step five. This gives unhurried time, which often results in a more creative engagement with the process.

Combining with the Angel of the Church Exercises

Another way of handling the material is to combine the Church Profile Exercise with engagement of the Angel of the Church Exercises as outlined in Chapter 12. Two particular ways of doing this are as follows.

One way is to take a Church Away Day from something like 10a.m. to 4p.m. and doing the Church Profile Exercise between 10a.m. and 1p.m. With a half-hour break (while the church profile is developed) this gives two and a half hours for the work. This slightly shorter time may well best be handled by leaving much of step five (taking action) to a future church council, or equivalent, meeting.

Then, after a shared lunch (allow 45 minutes), the angel material can be worked on. This works well as it is more visual and involves a fair amount of movement, which keeps people awake after lunch. This is further aided if a fifteen-minute tea break is built in at some point in the afternoon.

Another way of combining the Church Profile Exercise with the Angel of the Church Exercises has been pioneered particularly by the diocese of Rochester. It works in two stages as follows.

The first stage is for the incumbent or an external facilitator to introduce the marks of a healthy church and go as far as creating a church profile (step two) at an evening event.

The second stage takes place for four hours (typically 10a.m. to 3p.m.) on the following Saturday, or at least not more than ten days away from the first stage. At this day the facilitator divides the time in the following way:

- **first hour:** introducing and explaining the angel of the church and how it is possible to identify that angel. This concludes with the use of images of angels and a focus on the 'angel of present personality'.

- **second hour:** after further input on the concept of the angel of the church, work is done identifying the 'angel of vocation' for the church.

- **third hour:** working with the angel of present personality and the angel of vocation, the task is to identify what will be involved in moving from one to the other.

- **fourth hour:** this draws on both the work done earlier in the week on developing a church profile and the work done on the day to identify the journey from 'angel of personality' to 'angel of vocation'. Then the last three steps of the Church Profile Exercise (steps three to five) are done, ending up with some outline plans about how best to focus our efforts in developing the health of the church.

With images of Christ

David Brierley, the Canon Missioner of the Bradford diocese, has developed his own approach, which uses a variety of images and tactile forms to assist in the process. This includes using images of Christ to help people articulate the way they personally are energized by faith as well as to identify the Christ who is calling his Church today.

Varied applications of the *Healthy Churches* material

As the material has developed and spread more widely the ways that it is being used have diversified. Some dioceses have put the material to imaginative use in the following ways.

■ In one diocese the bishop's staff team decided they wanted to reduce the sense of 'distance' between the parishes and the 'centre' by having one senior staff member visiting every benefice. Having looked at a number of ways in which that might be handled, they decided to use the healthy churches material and invited each church to do the exercise prior to the visit. Out of this two-year process a diocesan strategy is being developed that builds on the insights of the healthy churches material with a view to getting it more fully into the lifeblood of the diocese and its thinking and way of working.

■ In other dioceses it has been found to be of particular value as something that all new incumbents are asked to do with their church during the second full year after their institution. At that stage they have some grasp of 'the angel of the church' but are still able to be somewhat objective about the situation that they have inherited more than created. It is a good time to do an exercise that will help the church set priorities about the things that really matter.

■ Other dioceses are using the material when churches are facing a vacancy. The argument used is that a church needs to know where it is going and what its priorities should be in the coming years before they can discern what sort of leader and leadership skills they should be looking for in their new incumbent.

■ Another diocese has started to use the material with churches where the prospect of having to close the church is becoming a real possibility. It helps to focus minds on what really needs to be done to turn this church around.

■ In several dioceses where the growing healthy churches programme has been in use, Archdeacon's Visitation questions have been used to find out the impact of the resource and the marks most needing attention in the diocese.

■ In at least two dioceses, the senior staff have sought external help to think through what is involved in 'growing a healthy diocese'.

■ In other dioceses, the healthy churches material has been introduced through Continuing Ministerial Education and Post-Ordination Training. The aim has been, quite consciously, to develop a 'healthy churches culture' in the diocese.

■ In some dioceses the effect of working on the healthy churches material has been to develop a united framework in which the sector ministers can all be involved and all refer churches to each other as different marks are found to need addressing.

No doubt the material will continue to be developed in other ways as it is used more widely but these patterns open up a range of different uses that apply not just to dioceses, or the Church of England, but to any grouping of churches.

Caring for the spirit in which the exercise is done

All that has been said in this book so far has sought to underline the importance of the way that a church manages its life. Indeed, the real difference between healthy and unhealthy churches is not in what they do but in the way that they do it.

The angel of the church perspective also reminds us that what really matters most is the spirit, ethos and feel of how a church operates, not just its organizational structures. Moreover, one of the best ways of helping a church to practise the marks of a healthy church is to enable it to engage in the Church Profile Exercise, energized by faith, with an outward-looking focus, seeking to find out what God wants, and so on.

So *how* the Church Profile Exercise is conducted really matters. Some of the things to pay attention to are as follows. Creating space for honest personal reflection is a great gift to give a church group. The work of reflecting can be stimulated by creating moments of silence and quiet space for reflection. So, for example, when the *Church Profile Sheet* is first shown, it is good to ask people to reflect in silence before engaging in any conversation. The honesty can be significantly stimulated by the facilitator's own honesty about themselves and their church and also by 'holding the ring' when participants are finding it difficult to express what they think to others who do not agree. So helping people to listen deeply to each other is a vital part of facilitating the process.

It is also very important to make sure that prayer and paying attention to God do not get squeezed out. It is not only good to begin and end days and sessions with prayer, but also to build pauses for prayer and meditation into the process. Very often a five- to ten-minute meditation at lunchtime, particularly on a whole day event, can be the highlight and most refreshing part of the exercise. In view of the amount of talking that will have gone on, the use of some visual aid, piece of music and simply silence can be more helpful than yet more words to add to the day.

In the final issue, it is also important to keep focused on the fact that the goal is discovering what action might best strengthen and develop the health of this church. Keeping our attention on God and on the people with whom we are working, together with the clear task, will greatly assist in enabling this exercise to be a blessing to individuals and of long-term value to the life and health of the church.

Study guide to healthy churches

It has been argued throughout this Handbook that the marks of a healthy church are expressions of the life of Christ in the local church. Engaging with the Scriptures can greatly aid our understanding and grasp of these marks.

The following study guide has been used in a number of ways as follows:

- **by groups** wishing to look at the marks more closely and relate them to the life of Christ and the life of the disciple;
- **by preachers:** particularly where a church is planning to do a series of sermons on the marks of a healthy church;
- **by facilitators:** as a helpful and informative background to leading a church through the Church Profile Exercise;
- **by individuals:** wishing to reflect on the marks of the healthy church as they relate both to their church and to their own Christian discipleship.

Mark 1: energized by faith

Study passages

Colossians 3.17
- What is special about the church?
- What kinds of change are we called to make?
- What kind of change might we need to make to be energized by faith?

Matthew 15.21-28: why did Jesus seem to be playing 'hard to get'?

Alternative passages
Luke 1.39-45: what on earth is happening here?
Micah 5.2-5 (and Galatians 4.19): what are we, as a church, meant to be pregnant with?

Meditation

The church is called on to embody the life of Jesus Christ who said

> *The Son can do nothing on his own, but only what he sees the Father doing. (John 5.19)*

Mark 2: outward-looking focus

Study passages

Luke 10.25-37

- What does it cost to be a Good Samaritan?
- Who are our 'neighbours' today?
- Who is calling out for our help in the world around us?

Isaiah 42.1-9: what is church for?

Meditation

The church is called to express the life of Jesus Christ, whose whole ministry was shaped by the conviction that

> *God so loved the world that he gave his only Son. (John 3.16)*

Mark 3: seeks to find out what God wants

Study passages

Luke 10.38 – 11.13

- What is Christianity, and so the church, about?
- What place do silence and reflection have in our life and church?
- What really matters in life?

Colossians 3.1-14: what sort of church might God want to join?

Meditation

The church is called to express the life of Jesus Christ who, as a child said

> *I must be in my Father's house. (Luke 2.49)*

Mark 4: faces the cost of change and growth

Study passages

Matthew 5.17-20

- Why do we find change so difficult?
- What needs changing?
- What helps us to change and be changed?
- Can you think of a change for the better that has taken place in your church and what lessons can we draw from that?

Exodus 18.13-27: what helps to bring about change?

Meditation

The church is called to express the life of Jesus Christ, who lived the truth that

> *Unless a grain of wheat fall into the earth and dies, it remains just a single grain; but if it dies, it bears much fruit. (John 12.24)*

Mark 5: operates as a community

Study passages

Ephesians 4.1-16 or 4.25 – 5.2

- So what makes for a healthy church, Paul?
- Do we all have to be the same?
- What is our part in contributing to a healthy church?

Mark 10.35-45: what can we do to build a healthy community?

Meditation

The church is called upon to embody the life of Jesus Christ who, having loved his own, loved them to the end and told us that

> *By this everyone will know that you are my disciples, if you have love for one another. (John 13.35)*

Mark 6: makes room for all

Study passages

Isaiah 65.17-25

■   What is God's agenda?

■   Who else is working on God's agenda?

■   How can we join in with what *they* are doing?

Matthew 8.1-8 (or 1-17): what on earth did he see in them?

Meditation

The church is called upon to embody the life of Jesus Christ, who told his disciples that

> *The Son of man came not to be served but to serve, and to give his life a ransom for many. (Matthew 20.28)*

Mark 7: does a few things and does them well

Study passages

Mark 1.14-15, and 21-39

■   What did Jesus see as his task and vocation?

■   Why is Jesus so clear about the job to be done?

■   And how can our lives, and our churches, follow that pattern?

Matthew 11.25-30: so why are we so busy?

Meditation

The church is called upon to embody the life of Jesus Christ of whom it was said

> *He has done everything well. (Mark 7.37)*

Chapter 11
The Church Profile Exercise

This chapter is a guide to running a Church Profile Exercise. It contains a detailed outline of the Church Profile Exercise. Figure 3 gives a visual overview of the process. Also included is a shortened version (90 minutes). It will repay careful study by anyone involved in running such an exercise.

The material has been 'road tested' and is designed to be as accessible as possible. However, there is no substitute for actually doing the exercise with a church and making the material your own; adapting as you judge best.

Timings are built around three one-hour sessions with suggested timings for each element within those sessions. They are simply advisory but are the fruit of experience in running this exercise. Session one is often the most difficult one to keep to one hour. Some time can be gained by shortening the other sections but too much shortening stifles creative conversation and so reduces the value of the exercise.

Detailed outline

All that follows should be read not as invariable rules but rather as guidance born of experience. Some may want to depart from some of the instructions given below right from the first time of using this material. Others may prefer to work initially with the material more or less as it is set out and then develop their own variations as they find out what works best for them.

Timings should be read as *advisory* not *mandatory*.

They are included, particularly for those new to this material, to give an indication of the amount of time that others have found helpful to allow for each stage. Another value of such timing is that it enables anyone leading the process to be aware of whether they have time available or if they need to speed up the process.

Timings in bold print (e.g. **15 mins**) are for a whole section; timings in italics (e.g. *3 mins*) are for each part of the section.

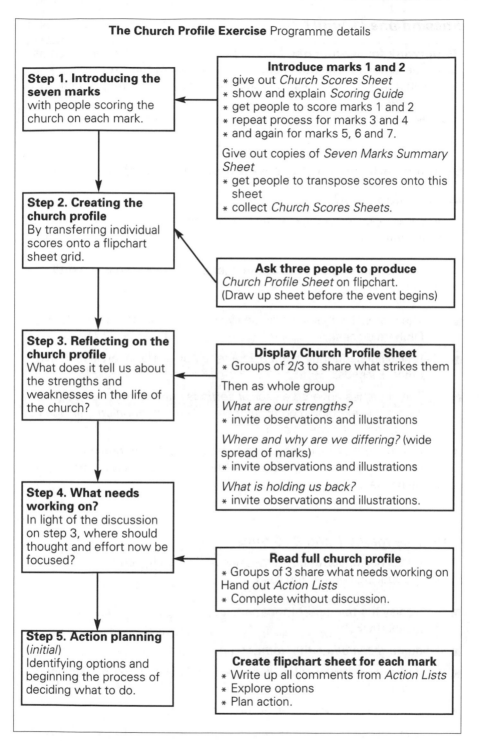

The Church Profile Exercise Programme details

Step 1. Introducing the seven marks
with people scoring the church on each mark.

Introduce marks 1 and 2
* give out *Church Scores Sheet*
* show and explain *Scoring Guide*
* get people to score marks 1 and 2
* repeat process for marks 3 and 4
* and again for marks 5, 6 and 7.

Give out copies of *Seven Marks Summary Sheet*
* get people to transpose scores onto this sheet
* collect *Church Scores Sheets*.

Step 2. Creating the church profile
By transferring individual scores onto a flipchart sheet grid.

Ask three people to produce
Church Profile Sheet on flipchart.
(Draw up sheet before the event begins)

Step 3. Reflecting on the church profile
What does it tell us about the strengths and weaknesses in the life of the church?

Display Church Profile Sheet
* Groups of 2/3 to share what strikes them

Then as whole group

What are our strengths?
* invite observations and illustrations

Where and why are we differing? (wide spread of marks)
* invite observations and illustrations

What is holding us back?
* invite observations and illustrations.

Step 4. What needs working on?
In light of the discussion on step 3, where should thought and effort now be focused?

Read full church profile
* Groups of 3 share what needs working on
Hand out *Action Lists*
* Complete without discussion.

Step 5. Action planning
(*initial*)
Identifying options and beginning the process of deciding what to do.

Create flipchart sheet for each mark
* Write up all comments from *Action Lists*
* Explore options
* Plan action.

Figure 3: The five steps of the Church Profile Exercise

Session one (1 hour)

Paperwork for session one (See Appendices for photocopiable copies of all the paperwork needed here and in the rest of the exercise.)
On flipchart/OHP: titles (only) of each mark, *Scoring Guide, Church Profile Sheet.*
For each participant: *Church Scores Sheet, Seven Marks Summary Sheet.*

Step one: introducing the seven marks (30–40mins)

Introduction (5–10 mins)

Welcome people, including consultant/facilitator – if one is being used, and open with prayer.

Introduce background/purpose of the exercise. In doing so it is worth making the following points:

■   The material is based on an analysis of growing churches in the Durham diocese.

■   It was subsequently refined as a result of similar exercises in five other dioceses.

■   The churches covered *all social settings* (rural, urban, suburban, city centre and ex-mining communities), *all church traditions, all ages of clergy,* and *all sizes of church.*

■   It is the fruit of research about what is actually happening in churches rather than based on a 'theory' about what ought to be happening.

Pray.

Introduce marks 1 and 2 (6 mins)

Some guidelines on introducing the marks of a healthy church.
When introducing each of the marks:

■   display the *title only* of the mark (e.g. *Energized by faith*) on a flipchart/OHP;

■   quote *the subtitle* (the '*rather than*' text);

■   introduce *a few of the bullet points* as 'what you might well find in a healthy church are . . .';

■   then read out some or all of the *bullet points;*

■   illustrate*:* the mark/bullet points with one or two stories of 'how this works out in some other churches'.

It has been found important not to show people all the written bullet points at this stage as it tends to give information overload. What needs to stay in their minds is what is meant by 'energized by faith', 'outward-looking focus', etc.

After introducing these first two marks:
Give out copies of the *Church Scores Sheet* (Appendix 1) to each person.

Ask people not to start scoring until after these instructions:

■   score what *you* think, not what you think others might think;

■   do not confer with others: we want to know what *you* think;

■   remember this is all *anonymous*;

■   use *the full range* of scores, avoid playing safe or being polite;

■   *score only the first two marks at this stage*;

■   score by putting a *circle* round the appropriate number.

Display the *Scoring Guide* (Appendix 2) on flipchart/OHP.
Allow time for instructions and scoring *(3 mins)*.

Introduce marks 3 and 4 (5 mins)

Repeat the instructions for scoring given above.
(Note: an alternative pattern is to do the scoring after the third and seventh marks only.) Then ask *people to score these next two marks only (2 mins)*.

Introduce marks 5, 6 and 7 (8 mins)

Repeat the instructions for scoring given above.
Then ask people to score *these last three marks (1 min)*.

Collecting in the Church Scores Sheets (5 mins)

When people have completed their scoring:

■   *give out* copies of the *Seven Marks Summary Sheet* (Appendix 4);

■   *invite them to copy* their score onto this Summary Sheet;
        (Explain that the reason for doing so is that you will shortly ask
        them to hand in their *Church Scores Sheet* so that a church profile
        can be developed. They need a record of what they scored for each
        mark. Put their score against each mark on the *Seven Marks
        Summary Sheet*.)

■   *collect* in *Church Scores Sheets* in order to create the Church Profile.

Note: Handing in sheets, rather than getting people to shout out their scores, has proved quite important as people tend to 'adjust' their scores in the light of what they hear others saying. They may be embarrassed by how low (or high) they have scored the church.

Proceed *to create the church profile* during the break between sessions.

Between session one and session two

Step two: creating the church profile (10–25 mins)

Filling in the Church Profile Sheet (Appendix 3) (10 mins)

With such help as has previously been suggested (see 'Helpers' section on pp. 110–111 above) complete the *Church Profile Sheet* bearing the following points in mind:

■ Use a bold felt tip pen: black is best for visibility.

■ Put one *tick* for each person's score. So if eight people have scored a mark as '2', do not write up '8' in the '2' column, but put *eight clear ticks*. Ticks give a clear visual pattern. See Figure 2b below. The Total column (see below) gives a numerical indicator.

■ If there are more than 30 people, forward planning will be needed to work out how best to transpose scores (using percentages is one way).

Normally this work is done by a small group during a break. However, if no break is taking place, it is important to do this work out of sight of church

Mark	1 low	2	3	4	5	6 high	Total
1. Energized by faith			✓✓✓	✓✓	✓		
2. Outward-looking focus	✓	✓	✓✓	✓	✓		
3. Seeks to find out what God wants			✓✓✓	✓✓✓			
4. Faces the cost of change and growth	✓	✓✓	✓✓	✓			
5. Operates as a community			✓✓	✓✓	✓	✓	
6. Makes room for all	✓✓	✓	✓✓✓				
7. Does a few things and does them well		✓✓✓	✓✓	✓			

Figure 2b: Entering scores on the Church Profile Sheet

members either by doing it at the back of the room or by turning the board so its back faces the group. Otherwise people will be distracted from whatever other task they have been moved on to.

Completing the Total column (see Figure 2c below) (10 mins)

This numerical approach is used, as some people find it easier to read a score visually (through the balance of where the ticks fall) whilst others find it more helpful to have a list of numbers from which they can immediately see high and low scores.

Two scoring methods are suggested below, but others can no doubt be created.

Points approach
For each mark:

- score 1 for every tick in the '1' column;
- score 2 for every tick in the '2' column, and so on;
- add the total points for the mark;
- put this total in the *Total* box against the mark.

See Table 1 on p. 126, where the totals for the marks are 36 and 45

Note: It is important to check that there is the same number of ticks against each of the seven marks, otherwise the scoring will be distorted. The reason for using this method of scoring is that, unless the scores are graded in some such way, the total will simply be the number of scores, which should be the same.

Mark	1 low	2	3	4	5	6 high	Total
1. Energized by faith			✓✓✓	✓✓	✓		22
2. Outward-looking focus	✓	✓	✓✓	✓	✓		18
3. Seeks to find out what God wants			✓✓✓	✓✓✓			21
4. Faces the cost of change and growth	✓	✓✓	✓✓	✓			15
5. Operates as a community			✓✓	✓✓	✓	✓	25
6. Makes room for all	✓✓	✓	✓✓✓				13
7. Does a few things and does them well		✓✓✓	✓✓	✓			16

Figure 2c: Completing the Total column

Mark	1	2	3	4	5	6	Total
energized by faith	0	2	4	5	–	–	36
outward-looking focus	0	1	3	2	4	1	45

Table 1

'Goal difference' approach

This approach is particularly suitable when there is a large number of people in the group or when time is very limited.

For each mark:

■   add up the total of scores for 4–6 points;

■   subtract from that sum the total of scores for 1–3 points;

■   put this figure in the Total column.

See Table 2 below, where the 'goal difference' for the marks is –1 and +3

Mark	1	2	3	4	5	6	Total
energized by faith	0	2	4	5	–	–	–1
outward-looking focus	0	1	3	2	4	1	+3

Table 2

Session two (1 hour)

Paperwork for session two
On flipchart/OHP: the completed Church Profile Sheet.
For each participant: *Action List* (Appendix 5).

Part one
Step three: reflecting on the church profile (25–35 mins)

This is done as a whole group with the *Church Profile Sheet* displayed on a flipchart where all can see it.

To stimulate discussion by the whole group it is useful to begin by asking people, in groups of two or three, to share what strikes them most from the *Church Profile Sheet* (4–5 mins).

Then, as a whole group get them to consider…

What are our strengths? (*7–10 mins*)
This can be 'read off' from the *Church Profile Sheet*.

■ *visually*, from where the majority of ticks are placed

■ *numerically* from the *Total* column.

Get the group to make their own observations rather than giving them your answers. Some churches find it difficult to admit anything is a strength and others find it hard to own up to weaknesses. It is as true for churches as it is for individuals that maturity (health) is evidenced by an ability to be realistic about both our gifts and our weaknesses.

Sometimes members of a church will never have talked like this before so it is important to be sensitive both to some awkwardness as well as to the excitement and a sense of relief that 'at last we can be honest with one another'. This may be particularly true about the church members' relation with the leader(ship), where they have not felt able to express their own, or a contrary, view.

One of the best ways of drawing insights out of people is, whenever some comment is made about strengths or weaknesses, to ask the person if they can illustrate the point they are making with a story from their experience.

If time allows, it can be very instructive to ask the further question: 'how did our strengths come to be so?' There are not necessarily easy or obvious answers, yet finding answers can help point a church to what may be involved in addressing what is holding us back.

> **One church, for example, after considerable thought, reckoned that all the moves forward in the life of the church in the previous 20 years had started with a vision held by one or two church members. That vision then spread to others, was sustained and got into the lifeblood of the church. Their sober reckoning was that such developments usually took the best part of ten years to come to maturity and produce evident fruit. They instanced the way the church had changed from being a church with 50 adults and no children or young people to 60 adults and 50 children or young people. It was a great change but it took twelve years.**

Just raising this question and inviting immediate answers for a couple of minutes can be instructive. It is also useful to say that this is something to leave the group to chew over in the coming weeks.

Where are we differing? (*7–10 mins*)

It is important to look at any mark where there is a wide spread of scores. There are several reasons for such situations.

It may be because people are looking at different aspects of the same issue. For example, a high score in *Outward-looking focus* might be because of the level of overseas missionary support, while a low score might be because of the weakness of the church's engagement with mission locally. Equally, a high score for *Operates as a community* may be the perspective of those who are members of a home group while a low score may come from those who are not currently members of such a group.

Another reason for a wide spread of scores may indicate differences of opinion that have not previously been addressed or have been suppressed because of fear of conflict. It is important to get these out in the open even if some of that conflict begins to become apparent. This may be a very valuable opportunity to help the group be honest about differences, hear what each other is saying, and be able to live with differences. If major differences emerge, however, it is best to get the group to note this as something to address in due course, but not to be diverted from doing the exercise by having a major debate on a thorny theological issue at this stage.

What is holding us back? (*7–10 mins*)

This is where we need to look at the marks with lower scores.

Once the obvious points have been made about lower scores, it is helpful to unpack this further by asking such questions as:

- where do we see evidence of this in the life of our church?
- has this always been the case?
- if so, why do you think this happened?
- if not, what has contributed to it being so?

Session two

Part two
Step four: what needs working on? (15 mins)

Step three involved a general reflection on strengths and weaknesses. Now the task is to identify specific areas for action and to develop plans for addressing the issues identified.

Explain that we are now going to think about what needs working on.

Ask people to turn back to the *Seven Marks Summary Sheet*, which was handed out during step one above. Ask people to read it through with a view to identifying which mark(s) seems to them most in need of attention at present (*2 mins*).

In groups of three, get people to share ideas about 'what needs working on' (*5 mins*).

Hand out the *Action Lists* sheets. Ask people to fill in their forms without further consultation with each other, in the light of the following instructions (*5 mins*).

From what you have heard, and thought about so far, what do you think we most need to work on? To answer this:

- Identify the *mark* you think needs addressing (suggest a maximum of two marks).
- If you identify with one or more of the *bullet points* put down the words in italics (e.g. *'motivation'* or *'nurturing faith'* under the first mark).
- If none of the bullet points express what you think, then add *your own words* – in a single phrase or sentence. For example, the real issue that may have emerged is *listening to the community*, *developing our welcome* or strengthening our *corporate prayer l ife*. In which case those are the key points people should put down on their *Action List*.

Tell people you want to collect in their *Action Lists*, so if they want to make a note of what they have put there, they need to copy it onto the *Seven Marks Summary Sheet*, noting ideas against the appropriate mark, before handing it in (*3 mins*).

The next task is to create corporate lists out of the *Action Lists* handed in. This is best done during a break. If no break is being taken, then a general discussion about 'so what do you think we need to work on?' should take place while the corporate lists are being developed.

Creating lists (between sessions)

- Create flipchart sheets, one for each mark, with the title of the mark (e.g. *Makes room for all*) on the top of the sheet.
- Write up every comment from the returned *Action Lists* sheets.
- Where a bullet point is mentioned (e.g. 'motivation' under the first mark), it is only necessary to put the key words – the ones in italics – on the list.
- Where there are repeats, put a tick for each repeat next to the point.

Then display these lists around the room. The normal situation at this point is that not every mark has something against it. This helps to narrow down the options. Often there are a few marks or themes that score widely whilst many points are mentioned only once or twice. It should, therefore, be possible to isolate no more than three or four areas for the whole group to explore.

Session three (1 hour)

> **Paperwork for session three**
> On flipchart sheets around the room: title of each mark with all comments from *Action Lists* entered (see session two, above). For groups: blank flipchart sheets for lists of possible actions.

Step five: action planning

Exploring options (45 mins)

The task now is to do some initial planning work on the key areas requiring attention that will be emerging from the work done in step four.
The suggested way of proceeding at this point is as follows:

- *Give people time to read the lists.* If at all possible, let them *walk around* to read the lists and identify the key issues needing attention. In such a 'walkabout' useful conversations may often take place (*5 mins*).

- *Invite general comments* (*5 mins*).

- *As a whole group* identify the *three or four areas* that emerge as the key issues that need to be addressed (*5 mins*).

- *Let people form self-selected groups to work on any of the issues.* If an area, previously identified, does not have anyone wanting to work on it, note it for future consideration. If the groups are unbalanced in size, that does not matter. However, if a large number of people – say, over ten – all want to work on one issue, then it is good to ask them to divide into two groups.

- Ask the groups to identify *what action could be taken.* Ask groups to make a list of all the things that could possibly be considered. The task is to generate as many ideas as possible, not to spend time discussing or evaluating them at this stage (*15 mins*).

- Then invite them to put their ideas down on a flipchart sheet to be displayed *when their list is complete* (*5 mins*).

■ Finally, ask each group to come up with one practical suggestion of the appropriate first step to be taken in developing this aspect of the life of the church, which they have been considering (*10 mins*).

Conclusion (15 mins)

It is important to make clear that this meeting is not the place to make any final plans because there needs to be time to reflect on all that has been said and as there are probably other decision-making bodies in the life of the church who have that responsibility.

However, it is good to give people opportunity to comment on what they have felt about the exercise and what are the implications for us as a church in the light of what we have done.

It is also good to explain as clearly as possible what will be done about the work that people have done together and on the likely timescale for any action on the issues raised. It is good also to say how the whole church will be informed about this meeting, how it went and about plans that, it is hoped, will emerge.

Time in silence to reflect personally on the process is a helpful way of ending.

This is often a good place at which to point out that maybe the reason why these seven marks are the marks of a healthy church is because they reflect the life of Christ. He was the One supremely who was *energized by faith, had an outward-looking faith, sought to find out what God wanted,* and so on.

Moreover, this means that this is a map not only for how the church should order its life, but also how we should live. We are called to be those who in following Christ are *energized by faith, have an outward-looking faith, seek to find out what God wants,* and so on.

Closing prayer and depart.

90-minute version of the exercise

It is possible to do the complete exercise in 90 minutes, for example at an evening meeting. To do so, follow the directions below.

Step one: introducing the seven marks (35 mins)

- Keep the *Welcome/introduction/prayer* to five minutes.
- Limit the introduction of each mark to three minutes.
- Do not read out the bullet points in introducing the marks.
- Hand out *Church Score Sheets* (Appendix 1) at the end, giving instructions for scoring at this point.
- Show *Scoring Guide* (Appendix 2) and get people to score all marks at this point.

Step two: creating the church profile (inside 10 mins)

- Have people set up ready to create the *Church Profile Sheet* (Appendix 3).
- *In groups of three:* get people to share what has struck them most about the life of the church by doing this exercise so far.
- *If Church Profile Sheet is not yet ready:* start exploring with the group *'what needs working on'*.

As soon as the church profile is ready proceed to the next step.

Step three: reflecting on the church profile (20 mins)

- Keep the discussions on *strengths*, *differences*, and *what is holding us back* to no more than 6 minutes each.

Step four: what needs working on? (10–15 mins)

- General discussion, without use of *Action Lists*.

Step five: action planning (10–15 mins)

- Say that all the ideas will be *presented* at the next meeting.
- Explain that now is not the time for *decision making* . . .
- but it would help to *get the feel* of what we are thinking.
- Invite people to share *one key action* they see as important.

Invite a variety of contributions, do not allow discussion about individual points: rather get out as many ideas as possible.

End the meeting with *thanks* for all those who have taken part, the *promise of returning to the issues* raised, and *prayer*.

Chapter 12
Angel of the Church Exercises

This chapter sets out three ways of working with the concept of the angel of the church.

■ **Working with images of angels:** using images of angels as the primary means of engaging with the subject.

■ **Other ways of working:** alternative approaches without the need for a collection of images of angels.

■ **Naming the angel of the church:** a variety of ways in which churches can discern the angel of their church.

The three elements can stand alone, work as pairs, or be woven together as is appropriate to the situation.

Working with images of angels

The chapter on the angel of the church (Chapter 9 above) is essential background to this exercise. If time and opportunity allow, reading the relevant chapter in Walter Wink's book[1] on which this exercise is based will provide further helpful background.

Working with the concept of the angel of the church is unfamiliar territory to most people. It therefore needs some introduction and explanation. It has also been found helpful to do some preliminary exercises (see below under 'warm-up exercises') to help people work in this more intuitive and imaginative way. Doing these preliminary exercises has proved more helpful than jumping straight into working with images of angels. Having said that, it can also be reported that most people have found the process enjoyable and energizing.

Warm-up exercises

Where several churches are involved it is good to get people to work in a group of three with no one else from their church in it. That makes it easier for people to speak their mind without having to consider whether other members of the church agree with them. Where there is just one church it is still good to work in groups of three people.

What sort of animal is your church like? Some of the things people have said are:

■ 'Our church is like an *elephant*: it never forgets, is very slow to move and very unpredictable as to which direction it might take when it does move.'

■ 'Our church is like a well-domesticated ageing *cat*: it is not at all frightening, is silky smooth to touch, and rarely stirs, as everything it needs is handed to it on a plate.'

■ 'Our church is like a *sheep dog*: it is well disciplined, barks a lot and most enjoys trying to get everyone to go where it wants them to.'

What colour is your church? This is not so easy but can uncover some very interesting insights into the nature of the church. It is important to underline, at least twice, that this question does not mean 'what is the predominant colour of your church *building*', but rather what colour speaks about the life of your church. Some of the illuminating responses have been:

■ 'Our church is *light green*': this was a recent 'church plant' that had the feel of spring growth about it. Interestingly, this was the colour chosen by two church members, *working in different groups*. It is not unknown for such similarities to emerge in these exercises.

■ 'Our church is *bright beige*': this delightful answer was explained by someone as 'our church has little of any interest or vitality about it most of the time when it fades into the background of the community around it, but every once in a while it stirs itself and does something really good and then it shines'.

■ 'Our church is *faded pink*: it would be "pretty" if it was not so tired, but there is nothing very robust or industrious about it.'

What is your church like? (a simile – 'our church is like . . .) This is more difficult still and people cannot always think of something but nonetheless it can be very productive to explore. Some of the images that have arisen are:

■ 'Our church is like a *wheelbarrow*: nothing moves unless you push it.'

■ 'Our church is like *a shop window* with nothing in it': a painfully honest insight that enabled the church to address the vacuum in the area of its spirituality.

■ 'Our church is like a *boat*': the person went on to amplify this by saying 'some people are rowing very hard but not making much progress, because others do not like the direction the boat is going in so are back-rowing, while others are not rowing at all, but only interested in painting the inside of the boat. Yet others are simply trying to find how to make it to the shore.'

■ 'Our church is a *jazz* church: there are common and repeated themes that we are all familiar with but you can never quite tell where the harmonizing will go on to next. There is plenty of participation and plenty of surprising developments coming from almost anywhere in the life of the church.'

The angel images exercise

An obvious minimum requirement is some images of angels. One way to start making a collection is to buy a copy of the book *Angels*.[2] It has 22 full-page woodcut illustrations of biblical encounters with angels. Art galleries, books, Christmas and other greetings cards and churches are further sources from which a collection can be built.

As a rule of thumb it is good to have at least twice as many images as there are likely to be people at the event.

Make sure tables are available and the room is big enough to cope not only with people sitting on chairs for part of the time but also sufficient room to put out tables for the angel images, with room enough for people to wander around those tables. As a guide, a six-foot table is enough room for about 20 images. It works best if the tables are spread widely around the available space rather than put all in one area. Doing so increases the circulating space and thus the number of people who can see the images at any one moment. The floor can be used to put out the images of angels but it needs to be borne in mind that elderly people may find it difficult to pick up an image from the floor.

Some points worth making by way of introduction to the exercise are:

■ There is no hurry about this exercise. Take time, you will not be rushed.

■ Do not take any image away from the tables *at this stage*. We will tell you when you can.

■ Enjoy this in the first place simply as an art exhibition. There is a wide range of different images, some of which are disturbing; a good number of them will bring a smile to your face. Some are a puzzle to makes sense of; others are quite beautiful.

■ When it comes to choosing an image, try to separate out your *enjoyment* of the pictures and your *choosing* one that best represents the personality or vocation of your church. You may love the Rembrandt or the Gauguin, but it may be the gaudy Christmas card that is a better expression of the life of your church at present.

■ Be open to the possibility that *an angel may choose you*. Be ready for some image, even a surprising, puzzling and not immediately clear image, to grab you. Let it.

Angel of personality

Briefly remind people that the angel of personality is about *present reality*. It is about how you see the church, as it is, warts and all, now. Do not think 'I wonder what the vicar thinks', or 'perhaps the church would not see it that way'. Nor, at this stage, should we be thinking about what we would like to be true of the church. The task is to choose an image that expresses *how you see the church at present*. Ask people to do this on their own and not to confer with other church members. The value is in each person choosing an image that speaks to them, not one that has been influenced by the thoughts of others.

Allow time for people to wander around the images. The amount of time will depend on the size of the group, but something like ten minutes is usually sufficient. Then ask people to pick up one image and return to their seat, back into the group of three from which they came.

It is helpful to say that, if more than one person wishes to choose the same image, then they need to arrange for one to share the image first in their group and then hand it over for the other person to share it last in their group. Alternatively, someone may be willing to choose another, similar, image.

Ask people to remain silent when they return to their seat and to reflect on the image they have picked up and why it speaks to them of their church.

When everyone is back in their seats, invite them to share why they have chosen that particular one. The task of those sitting around is not to comment on the choice or agree or disagree but rather to help the person speaking to identify ways in which the image speaks to them about their church.

It is important to give people enough time for this sharing (ten minutes is again about the right amount of time if people are in threes). Alert people two or three minutes before the end of this time as to how long they have so that, if someone has not had an opportunity to share their image, they can do so in the remaining time.

At the end of this stage it is important to get the images back on the tables for the next part of the process.

Angel of vocation

The next step is to move on to consider the angel of vocation. In introducing this, the vital point to make is that the task now is to give expression to our imagination, hopes, dreams, longings, prayers. This is about choosing an angel that expresses something of what you see the church *called to become* and/or *do*.

Remind people . . .

- not to discuss this at this stage with other church members;
- not to pick up an image until invited to do so;
- to be open to an angel 'choosing you'.

Where time allows, after people have shared why they have chosen this image, invite them to help each other think about what steps their church might need to take to move towards that sort of vocation.

When working with a number of churches, and if time allows, people can then move into their church groups and share their 'angel of vocation' with each other. They can then be asked to consider what this exercise suggests will be needed to move from 'the angel of present personality' to 'the angel of vocation'.

Particularly if energy levels are dropping, for example in an after lunch session, it is instructive, fun and energizing to get a church group to decide which of the various images of the angel of vocation best expresses what God is calling the church to become. For this to work, people need to be ready to argue for their image rather than all defer to the one chosen by the minister!

Other ways of working

Drawing a picture that represents your church. One person who did so drew an elderly couple sitting in a bungalow watching television while, outside, in a nearby playing field, large numbers of children were obviously enjoying themselves. There was no path between the two groups.

Sculpture. Using pottery clay or even play-dough to create something that expresses what you understand God is calling this church to become.

Body sculpture. If you have six or more people from a church, get them to form some shape together that expresses what they see as their sense of God's vocation for this church.

Playlet. A group of at least six is probably needed to make this work. The brief here is to think ahead, say five years, and imagine what would be happening if the vocation and vision we have been sharing had come into being. What would be happening? The group then develops a five or so minute 'playlet' illustrating this vocation happening.

Images of Christ.[3] Where there is access to images of Christ rather than images of angels it is possible to use them in a way similar to the angel images. In this case the first question, relating to the angel of present personality, would be something like: 'who is the Christ this church most easily recognizes at present?' For the angel of vocation the question might be 'who is the Christ we are being called to follow?'

Naming the angel of the church

There are a number of ways in which a church can set about identifying its angel. Some of the most accessible ways are set out below. They are not the only ways but they indicate a range of possibilities.

The 'characteristics' approach

The idea here is to identify some key words, or characteristics, of a church that help to describe its essence. The goal is to identify three or so words that best describe the current spirit and feel of the church.

One way of doing this with a larger group, such as a church council, is as follows.

- Introduce the exercise by saying that the aim is to understand the church, as a living entity, better.
- Invite individuals to name a characteristic of a wider grouping, whether Manchester United, the diocese, or a major local employer. This gets people into this way of thinking and helps them to relax, as the answers do not matter greatly.
- Ask people, either individually or in groups of no more than three, to identify not more than five words that best describe the nature of this church.
- Put each characteristic on a postcard-sized sticky note and ask people to put those up on a flipchart sheet or wall (if a flipchart sheet is not big enough).
- Get the whole group to move the notes around so that they are grouped together under common themes or headings. Let people do the sorting, even if it feels like chaos. Do not have someone up

front doing it for them. As themes become clear, write them in felt-tip on the flipchart sheets above the groupings of sticky notes. Look for some key themes to emerge.

Once some key characteristics have been identified, then consider how each one needs to be nourished, if it is a healthy characteristic, or addressed, if it is unhealthy.

The 'descriptive' approach

The aim here is to write a description, rather like the one quote above of BBC North written by the Revd Angela Tilby (see page 97). This work can be done by inviting either written or verbal contributions that they see as describing the personality/angel of this church. Though a lot less tidy and not so easy to get hold of, this may well yield a richer description of the angel of the church.

Another way of using this same approach is to write, or invite people to write, a letter from the risen Christ to 'the angel of the church in ...' using the framework for such a letter set out on pages 92–3 above.

An 'exploratory' approach

This is the approach outlined by Walter Wink himself. He suggests among other places to look for signs of the angel of a church are:

- The architecture and ambience.
- The economic class and income of its members.
- A church's power structures.
- How the church handles conflict.

An outline for this approach is set out in Appendix 6. This can be done by an individual, though a richer picture emerges if a number of people complete this sort of pro forma and someone then works to create a corporate one, drawing on as many of the insights from the individual ones as possible.

The suggested way of using this is to give people a copy of *Naming the Angel of the Church* (Appendix 6) inviting them, either on their own, with friends, home groups, or in whatever grouping they choose, to complete as many of the boxes as they have something to say about. Those sheets can then be pooled and the major themes be shared with a church council or in some wider way with the whole church.

The value of this approach is that it can take place over an extended time, in people's own time and in their natural groups. It does not need a day away, though an evening event at which the outcomes can be shared is likely to prove both valuable and interesting to all who have been involved. It could form a stimulating part of a church's Annual General Meeting.

Whatever approach is used, the greater the number of people involved the greater will be the value to the church and the more effect the whole exercise is likely to have. Certainly people are much more inclined to work to bring into being a vision and sense of direction for a church that they have had a hand in shaping than would be the case if a leader, or leadership group, simply declared 'here is the vision for our church'.

Being the church better

There are a number of benefits to taking the angels/intuitive approach to reflecting on the life of the church.

One is that it draws on people's creativity and imagination in a situation where our 'mental model' of church is often both tired and constraining. This intuitive approach can break through those unconscious constraints to our discerning what is appropriate and possible.

Another is that it helps people see the church as an entity, a whole, and to do so in a way that breaks out beyond the constraints of thinking of the church simply as an organization. This enables us to be in touch with a deeper dynamic that is always at work in any social structure, namely the feel, spirit and ethos of that structure.[4]

A further great value in taking this approach is that it draws a church's attention to what is often the major area where work needs to done to develop the health of a church, namely the being or essence of the church. We much more easily imagine that change will be about what we do, whereas the deepest changes are in who we are. Seeing the church as a whole, and grasping a vision of a church made whole, can lead us to focus on how we *are* church, not just on how we do church.

For many churches, identifying how we *are* church and how we could *be* church better is likely to prove the most fruitful, costly and creative outcome of engagement with the whole healthy churches process.

It is to that goal that this work is offered.

Appendix 1
Church Scores Sheet

circle the number you consider most appropriate

1. energized by faith
rather than just keeping things going or trying to survive

low   1   2   3   4   5   6   high

2. outward-looking focus
with a 'whole life' rather than 'church life' concern

low   1   2   3   4   5   6   high

3. seeks to find out what God wants
discerning the Spirit's leading rather than trying to please everyone

low   1   2   3   4   5   6   high

4. faces the cost of change and growth
rather than resisting change and fearing failure

low   1   2   3   4   5   6   high

5. operates as a community
rather than functioning as a club or religious organization

low   1   2   3   4   5   6   high

6. makes room for all
being inclusive rather than exclusive

low   1   2   3   4   5   6   high

7. does a few things and does them well
focused rather than frenetic

low   1   2   3   4   5   6   high

Scoring Guide

Scoring Guide

Circle the number that best
describes what *you* see
is happening in your church

1. weak and holding us back

2. only a few signs

3. some evidence of this

4. making progress

5. evidence of much of this

6. this is a strength

Church Profile Sheet

Mark	1 low	2	3	4	5	6 high	Total
1. Energized by faith							
2. Outward-looking focus							
3. Seeks to find out what God wants							
4. Faces the cost of change and growth							
5. Operates as a community							
6. Makes room for all							
7. Does a few things and does them well							

Seven Marks Summary Sheet

Mark 1: energized by faith

rather than just keeping things going or trying to survive

- *worship and sacramental life*: move people to experience God's love
- *motivation*: energy comes from a desire to serve God and one another
- *engages with Scripture*: in creative ways that connect with life
- *nurtures faith in Christ*: helping people to grow in, and share, their faith.

Mark 2: outward-looking focus

with a 'whole life' rather than a 'church life' concern

- deeply rooted in the *local community,* working in partnership with other denominations, faiths, secular groups and networks
- passionate and prophetic about *justice and peace*, locally and globally
- makes connections between *faith and daily living*
- responds to human need by *loving service.*

Mark 3: seeks to find out what God wants

discerning the Spirit's leading rather than trying to please everyone

- *vocation*: seeks to explore what God wants it to be and do
- *vision*: develops and communicates a shared sense of where it is going
- *mission priorities*: consciously sets both immediate and long-term goals
- able to call for, and make, *sacrifices,* personal and corporate, in bringing about the above and living out the faith.

Mark 4: faces the cost of change and growth

rather than resisting change and fearing failure

- while embracing the past, it dares to take on *new ways of doing things*

- *takes risks*: admits when things are not working, and learns from experience
- *crises*: responds creatively to challenges that face the church and community
- *positive experiences of change:* however small, are affirmed and built on.

Mark 5: operates as a community

rather than functioning as a club or religious organization

- *relationships*: are nurtured, often in small groups, so that people feel accepted and are helped to grow in faith and service
- *leadership*: lay and ordained work as a team to develop locally appropriate expressions of all seven marks of a healthy church
- *lay ministry*: the different gifts, experiences and faith journeys of all are valued and given expression in and beyond the life of the church.

Mark 6: makes room for all

being inclusive rather than exclusive

- *welcome*: works to include newcomers into the life of the church
- *children and young people:* are helped to belong, contribute and be nurtured in their faith
- *enquirers* are encouraged to explore and experience faith in Christ
- *diversities*: different social and ethnic backgrounds, mental and physical abilities, and ages, are seen as a strength.

Mark 7: does a few things and does them well

focused rather than frenetic

- *does the basics well*: especially public worship, pastoral care, stewardship and administration
- *occasional offices*: make sense of life and communicate faith
- *being good news* as a church in its attitudes and ways of working
- *enjoys what it does* and is relaxed about what is not being done.

Appendix 5
Action Lists

1. energized by faith

what needs working on..

....

2. outward-looking focus

what needs working on..

....

3. seeks to find out what God wants

what needs working on..

....

4. faces the cost of change and growth

what needs working on..

....

5. operates as a community

what needs working on..

....

6. makes room for all

what needs working on..

....

7. does a few things and does them well

what needs working on..

....

Appendix 6
Naming the Angel of the Church

The colour of our church is (church *life*, not *building*)

....

because ....

....

....

....

....

....

Our church building says

....

....

....

....

....

....

....

....

The local context/culture can best be described as (e.g. *fragmented, comfortable, friendly, frantic* ...)

....

....

....

....

The history of this church is a story of ....

....

....

....

....

What we are trying to do here is

· ·

· ·

· ·

· ·

· ·

· ·

· ·

The clergy/lay relationship can best be described as

· ·

· ·

· ·

· ·

· ·

· ·

What is missing in this church is

· ·

· ·

· ·

· ·

· ·

· ·

The best thing about this church is

· ·

· ·

· ·

· ·

· ·

· ·

The angel or personality of this church can best be described in terms of

· ·

· ·

· ·

· ·

Notes

Introduction

1 Robert Warren, *Building Missionary Congregations*, Church House Publishing, 1995.
2 Christian Schwarz, *Natural Church Development*, ChurchSmart Resources, 1996.
3 Ephesians 4.13.

Chapter 1

1 Christian Schwarz, *Natural Church Development*, ChurchSmart Resources, 1996.

Chapter 2

1 Gerard Hughes, *God of Surprises*, Darton, Longman & Todd, 1985, p. 22.
2 David J. Bosch, *Transforming Mission*, Orbis Books, 1991, p. 390.
3 Robin Greenwood, *Practising Community: The task of the local church*, SPCK, 1996, p. 64.
4 See www.alcoholics-anonymous.org.uk.
5 Acts 4.20.

Chapter 3

1 John 8.32.
2 Laurie Green, *Let's Do Theology*, Mowbrays, 1990, p. 103.
3 Matthew 11.28-30.
4 Romans 15.7.
5 Michael Fullan, *Change Forces*, The Falmer Press, 1993.
6 Loren Mead, *The Once and Future Church*, Alban Institute, 1991, p. 76.
7 Derek Baldwin, *Open Doors, Open Minds*, Highland, 1994.

Chapter 4

1 Michael Crosby, *Spirituality of the Beatitudes*, Orbis Books, 1992.

2 *Working as One Body*, Church House Publishing, 1995.
3 Michael Riddell, *Threshold of the Future*, SPCK, 1998, p. 155.
4 John Westerhoff III, *Living the Faith Community*, Harper & Row, 1985, p. 72.
5 Roberta Bondi, *To Pray and to Love*. Burns & Oates, 1991, p. 107.
6 John Adair, *The Leadership of Jesus and its Legacy Today*, Canterbury Press, 2001.
7 This is part of the thesis of Thomas R. Hawkins, *The Learning Congregation*, Westminster John Knox Press, 1997. One of the most helpful books on leadership for today's culture.
8 Comment made at a conference. He is the author of *The Isaiah Vision*, WCC Publications, 1992.
9 See *Contact* in the *Emmaus* material for a more detailed, and practical, exploration of this subject.
10 Bob Jackson, *Hope for the Church*, Church House Publishing, 2002.
11 Christian Schwarz, *Natural Church Development*, ChurchSmart Resources, 1996.

Chapter 5

1 Christian Schwarz, *Natural Church Development*, ChurchSmart Resources, 1996.

Chapter 6

1 For a full outline of this process see Marvin Weisbord and Sandra Janoff, *Future Search*, Berrett-Koehler Publishers, 1995.
2 Loren Mead, *The Once and Future Church*, Alban Institute, 1991, p. 80.
3 *Church for Others*, World Council of Churches, 1968.

Chapter 7

1 A classic work, though a substantial volume, is George Lovell, *Consultancy, Ministry and Mission*. Burns & Oates, 2000.

Chapter 8

1 Robert Warren, *Building Missionary Congregations*, Church House Publishing, 1995, p. 26.
2 Jürgen Moltmann, *The Open Church*, SCM Press, 1978, p. 6.
3 Robin Greenwood, *Practising Community*, SPCK, 1996, p. 64.

Chapter 9

1 Exodus 4.1-7.
2 James Hopewell, *Congregation: Stories and structures*, SCM Press, 1988.
3 Walter Wink, *Unmasking the Powers*, Fortress Press, 1986, is the particular one referred to later in the text.
4 Revelation 2.1-7.
5 Revelation 2.2-7.
6 Wink, *Unmasking the Powers*, p. 73.
7 Wink, *Unmasking the Powers*, p. 80.
8 Revelation 2.2-5.
9 From an unpublished address given in the Durham diocese in 1998.
10 William Vanstone, *The Stature of Waiting*, Darton, Longman & Todd, 1982.
11 Robin Greenwood, *Practising Community: The task of the local church*, SPCK, 1996, p. 28.

Chapter 12

1 Walter Wink, *Unmasking the Powers*, Fortress Press, 1986. Chapter 2: The angel of the church.
2 Adrian Roberts, woodcuts by Pauline Jacobsen, *Angels*, The Celtic Cross Press, 1998, available from Ovins Well House, Lastingham, York YO62 6TJ.
3 *The Christ We Share* pack (jointly produced by USPG, CMS and the Methodist Church) gives 32 images of Christ on cards and on acetates. It forms a good starting point for making a collection of images of Christ.
4 Ronald W. Richardson, *Creating a Healthier Church*, Fortress Press, 1996.

Resources for healthy churches

The list below contains some resources that have proved useful for churches seeking to develop their health. Although an indication is given of which of the seven marks of a healthy church each resource relates to, they can doubtless be of value in developing areas other than those indicated.

Repeated resources*

Some resources are referred to a number of times in the material. In order to avoid undue repetition, the full contact details of these resources are given in this section. In the detailed text this is indicated by an asterisk* at the end of the reference. These contact details are given here in alphabetical order.

Alban Institute, www.alban.org

CPAS (Church Pastoral Aid Society), Athena Drive, Tachbrook Park, Warwick, CV34 6NG; Tel: 01926 4548458; email: info@cpas.org.uk; www.cpas.org.uk

Continuum, International Publishing Group, The Tower Building, 11 York Road, London, SE1 7NX, Tel: 020 7922 0880, www.continuumbooks.com

LICC (The London Institute for Contemporary Christianity), Vere Street, London, W1G 0DQ; Tel: 020 7399 9555; email: mail@licc.org.uk; www.licc.org.uk

Grove Books, Grove Books Ltd, Ridley Hall Road, Cambridge, CB3 9HU; Tel: 01223 464748; www.grovebooks.co.uk

Matters Arising (formerly 'Administry'), for details contact Rob Norman, 62 Farm Road, Rowley Regis, West Midlands, B65 8ET. Low-cost local call telephone number: 0845 128 5177; email: mail@mattersarising.com; www.mattersarising.com

RUN (Reaching the Unchurched Network), PO Box 387, Aylesbury, Buckinghamshire, HP21 8WH; www.run.dbithell.co.uk*

York Courses, PO Box 343, York, YO19 5YB; Tel and Fax: 01904 481677; email: admin@yorkcourses.clara.co.uk

Overview

Mission-shaped Church, Church House Publishing, 2004 (General Synod report). Thorough overview of fresh expressions of church. Useful appendix of resources and contacts which complements the list supplied here.

Bob Jackson, *Hope for the Church*, Church House Publishing, 2002. Clear analysis of statistical evidence for trends of growth and decline in the life of the Church, with pointers to achievable actions to reverse decline. Touches on all the marks of a healthy church.

Steve Chalke and Sue Radford, *New Era, New Church?*, Harper Collins, 1999. Based on the ten pledges of 'The New Millennium Challenge to the

Churches'. It has some excellent practical material, of help in addressing any of the marks of a healthy church.

Jim Collins, *Good to Great*, Random House Business Books, 2001. Fascinating look at six characteristics of businesses that have moved from being good to being great. The author makes the point that 'if we have cracked the code on the question of good to great, we should have something of value to any type of organization. Good schools might become great schools ... *Good churches might become great churches*' (my italics).

Checking Your Church's Health, published by Administry 1999. See Matters Arising*.

Training Event: *Checking your Church's Health*, provided by Matters Arising*.
For a list of over ten other 'marks of vitality' see:
www.easumbandy.com/resources/index.php?action=details&record=200

Resources

Christian Schwarz, *Natural Church Development*, British Church Growth Association, 1996. A complementary approach to that of this handbook with many useful insights of relevance to either approach.

A Church without Walls, Church of Scotland, 2001, www.churchwithoutwalls.org.uk

Open all Hours, URC Thames North Synod. An interesting resource pack for churches based around ten marks of 'openness'. Available from 020 7799 5000 or office@urc10.org

Reaching the Unchurched Network applies insights from Willow Creek, working for churches 'passionate about: cultural relevance, spiritual encounter, creative excellence, relational community and visionary leadership', www.run.org.uk*

Christian Resources Exhibitions bring together over 500 companies, charities and mission organizations at exhibitions across the country. To find out details of forthcoming exhibitions call 01844 271476 or visit www.creonline.co.uk

Matters Arising has resources, including training events, built up over a number of years. A number of these are listed under various marks below. See Matters Arising*.

Grove Books have a wide range of 25 page booklets of a practical nature under a number of headings, including *Evangelism, Pastoral, Spirituality, Worship*, etc. See Grove Books*.

York Courses produces ecumenical study material for small groups on various aspects of the Faith. Courses include a booklet and audio tape/CD, with high profile Christian leaders participating on the tape/CD. Contributors include the Archbishops of Canterbury and York, the Bishop of Durham, Gerard Hughes, Frances Young and Steve Chalke. See York Courses*.

Assessing resources

Several publications have attempted to research the impact of currently available resources and to assess their strengths and weaknesses. These publications include:

Mike Booker and Mark Ireland, *Evangelism: Which Way Now?* Church House Publishing, 2003. A good range of resources and detailed assessment of many of them – including the *Healthy Churches* material. Helpful in assessing the relevance, strengths and weaknesses of much that follows in the list of resources.

Mike Booker, *Exploring Natural Church Development*, Grove Books*, 2001 (EV55).

Leadership, Vision and Growing Churches, Christian Research Association. This includes a detailed statistical analysis of a range of process evangelism resources. Available from Christian Research Association, Vision Building, 4 Footscray Road, Eltham, London SE9 2TZ (£1, including p & p). See www.christian-research.org.uk

Charles Freebury, *Alpha or Emmaus?* Detailed analysis and comparison. Available from Charles Freebury, 89 Hermitage Street, Crewkerne, Somerset, TA18 8EX; email: charles.freebury@tesco.net. £11.50 (20 Euros outside UK) includes p & p.

Context resources

Listed below are resources of particular relevance to churches in urban, suburban and rural contexts respectively. The resources each relate to a wide range of marks of a healthy church.

Urban context resources

The Churches' Community Work Alliance provides a regular newsletter as well as specific publications addressing issues of good practice associated with church related community work. Contact CCWA, St Chad's College, North Bailey, Durham, DH1 3RH; Tel: 0191 374 7342.

Materials produced by the Church of Scotland under the heading **UPA Resources**. These cover worship material and discipleship as well as community involvement. Contact The Church of Scotland Office for National Mission, 59 Elmbank Street, Glasgow, G2 4PQ; Tel: 0141 333 1948. Each pack costs around £3 and all the material is available for photocopying.

The Shaftesbury Society is producing booklets to summarize the learning and experience that can be gleaned from Shaftsbury's extensive community development projects throughout England. To get a list of publications available now and as they are produced contact Sue Hoey, The Shaftsbury Society, Jubilee Mill, North Street, Bradford, BD1 4EW; Tel: 01274 736618.

Community-led Regeneration and the Local Church, Samuel Wells, Grove Books*, 2003, (P94).

Called to the City, a four-part study pack for small groups produced by Church Mission Society (CMS). Details from: Tel: 020 7928 8681, email: sales@coms-uk.org; www.cms-uk.org

Andrew Davey, *Urban Christianity and Global Order*, SPCK, 2001. Andrew Davey is the Church of England's Urban Affairs Officer, based at Church House, Westminster.

Laurie Green, *Urban Ministry and the Kingdom of God*, SPCK, 2003. See also the resources details on page 153.

Unlock, see www.unlock-urban.org.uk
Urban Theology Unit, The Sheffield Federation of Centres for Biblical, Theological and Mission Studies, 210 Abbeyfield Road, Sheffield, S4 7AZ; Tel: 0114 243 5342.
National Estate Churches Network, contact Carol Potter, 36 Custom Street, London, SW1P 4AU.
Urban Ministry and Theology Project, Partnership Building, Welbeck Road, Walker, Newcastle upon Tyne, NE6 4JS, Tel: 0191 262 1680; Fax: 0191 295 4573; email: admin@umtp.org; www.umtp.org
Urban Bulletin, ECUM, Bethnal Green Mission Church, 305 Cambridge Heath Road, London, E2 9LH; Tel: 020 7729 6262; email: xpressanny@aol.com

Suburban context resources

Michael Gwilliam, *Sustainable Suburbs*, Joseph Rowntree Foundation, 1999.
Civic Trust Sustainable Suburbs Project, see www.civictrust.org.uk
R. D. Putnam, *Bowling Alone*, Simon & Schuster, 2000.
Richard Harries, *Is There a Gospel for the Rich?: The Gospel in a Capitalist World*, Continuum*, 1992.
Gibson Winter, *Suburban Captivity of the Churches*, Doubleday, 1961.
Newcastle/Winchester Consultation, *Faith in Suburbia?* Follow up pack available from Canon Geoff Miller, St Nicholas Cathedral, Newcastle upon Tyne, NE1 1PF.
Faith in Suburbia (P95), Jane Gibbs, Grove Books*, 2003.
Ann Morisy, *Journeying Out: A New Approach to Christian Mission*, Continuum*, 2004.

Rural context resources

The Arthur Rank Centre, an ecumenical body providing resources for the church in the rural context, including:

- *Country Way* magazine, three times a year on subscription;
- Books, especially ACORA publications, including, *Rural Ministry; Rural Visitors; Rural Youth*. Full booklist available on request.
- Courses in spring and autumn for ordained and lay people new to rural ministry; another specifically for those involved in multi-parish benefices; postgraduate courses with Centre for Studies in Rural Ministry, University of Wales, Bangor at St Deiniol's Library, Hawarden;
- Conferences for rural specialists;
- Briefing notes (via email and on web site) on farming and other rural issues;
- Support and networking on rural issues;
- Computer and furniture schemes for rural churches and organizations.

Contact: The Arthur Rank Centre, Stoneleigh Park, Warwickshire, CV8 2LZ; Tel: 024 7685 3060; email: info@arthurrankcentre.org.uk; www.arthurrankcentre.org.uk

Rural Theology Association: twice-yearly magazine *Rural Theology*;
newsletter; regional groups; national conferences.
Email: stephen.cope@dial.pipex.com; www.rural-theology.org.uk
Christian Rural Concern (CRuC): certificate and diploma courses validated
by Keele University; journal; day and weekend conferences.
Email: secretary@cres.org.uk; www.cres.org.uk
Rural Evangelism Network: coordinating several bodies specifically
committed to rural evangelism with the work of main Christian
denominations. Email: ren@ruralmissions.org.uk
Churches Tourism Association (not limited to rural churches): newsletter;
networking through web site, conferences.
Email: paul@churchestourismassociation.info,
enquire@churchestourismassociation.info; or
www.churchestourismassociation.info
Rural Sunrise: 'to enable and encourage churches to put mission
permanently on their agendas in ways that are biblical, appropriate and
effective'. Offers training, publications and resources. Including material for
work with children. For details see www.ruralmissions.org.uk/sunrise.htm
Geoff Treasure, *First the Blade*, CPAS*, 2003. Six interactive sessions on
the development of rural ministry. Available from CPAS* who also offer
consultancy for rural churches.
Richard Askew, *From Strangers to Pilgrims – Evangelism and the Church
Tourist*, Grove Books*, 1997 (EV38).

1. Energized by faith

Process evangelism courses

There are many now available. While their primary use is in communicating
the faith to 'enquirers' **(Marks 1 and 6)** they also work well in helping
existing church members to reflect on their faith, experience a refreshment
and renewal of that faith and enable them to articulate a previously
unarticulated faith.
Alpha, based on Nicky Gumbel's book, *Questions of Life*. For details contact
The Alpha Office, Holy Trinity Brompton, Brompton Road, London, SW7 1JA;
Tel: 0845 6447544; www.alphacourse.org
Michael Green, *After Alpha*, Kingsway, 1998.
Emmaus, Church House Publishing. Available from bookshops or directly
from Church House Bookshop, Tel: 020 7898 1300. Contact address:
Emmaus Coordinator, Church House Publishing, Church House, Great Smith
Street, London SW1P 3NZ. Note that a major part is the *Growth* section that
is specifically designed to help people grow in their faith. See
www.e-mmaus.org.uk
R. Tice and B. Cooper, *Christianity Explored*, Paternoster, 2002. Ten sessions
plus a week-end. Includes tapes and leader's manual. Available from All
Souls, Langham Place, London; Tel: 020 7580 3522. See
www.christianityexplored.com

Robin Gamble, *Start! Discovering Christianity in six small-group sessions*, CPAS*. This down-to-earth course assumes no previous knowledge of the Christian faith. Twelve location-based mini-videos open up the sessions' topics.
James Lawrence, Penny Frank and others, *Lost for Words: Sharing Faith Naturally*, CPAS*. Helps all ages find their voice and speak confidently about their faith. Features separate course material for adults, teenagers and children.
Rob Frost, *Essence: A six-session course for today's spiritual seekers*, Kingsway/CPAS*. An informal course for people who may look first to the 'New Age', rather than the Christian faith for spiritual refreshment. Companion CD includes music and meditations. **(Marks 1 and 6)**
The 'Y' Course, Meadows & Steinberg, BRF, 1999.
Journeys, produced by the Willow Creek Foundation (UK). Details from www.willowcreek.org.uk
Mike Booker and Mark Ireland, *Evangelism: Which Way Now?* Church House Publishing, 2003. Chapters 2–4 give a well-researched and well-balanced assessment of the various courses as well as advice on developing a locally grown one.
See also the Assessing Resources section above on pp.153–4.
John Drane, *Looking at Evangelism from the Inside Out*, Administry, 1997. See Matters Arising*.
John and Olive Drane, *Being Creative with Forms of Worship*, Administry, 2002. See Matters Arising*.
David Springs, *Living Spirituality*, Administry, 2001. See Matters Arising*.

Worship resources

New Patterns for Worship, Church House Publishing, 2002. Not just a wealth of liturgical material but also some helpful notes on the use of liturgy.
Michael Perham, *Liturgy Pastoral and Parochial*, SPCK, 1984.
Michael Perham, *Lively Sacrifice*, SPCK, 1992.
David Stancliffe, *God's Pattern: Shaping Our Worship, Ministry and Life*, SPCK, 2003.
Praxis, was formed in 1990 as an initiative in liturgical formation for the Church of England sponsored by the Liturgical Commission of the Church of England, the Alcuin Club, and the Group for the Renewal of Worship. See www.praxisworship.org.uk

Spirituality movements

Cursillo, 'A movement of the Church providing a method by which Christians are empowered to grow through prayer, study and action and enabled to share God's love with everyone'. Contact address: British Anglican Cursillo Council, 1 Kirby Close, Brandon, Coventry, CV8 3HZ; **www.ukcursillo.org (Mark 1 and 3)**
Focolare, the Focolare movement came into being when Chiara Lubich and her friends started trying to live the Gospel'. See www.rc.net/focolare **(Mark 1 and 3)**

Renovaré (a Latin word meaning 'to renew') 'was founded by Richard J. Foster as an initiative working for the renewal of the Church, drawing on a wide variety of experience in the teaching and practice of discipleship and spiritual formation. through conferences, retreats, workshops and writing'. See www.renovare.org.uk **(Mark 1 and 3)**

While these are essentially suitable for individuals to engage with any church can encourage members to participate in them and draw insights from them that can be of relevance to the life of the church.

Retreats and retreat centres

Retreats magazine gives details of centres and courses. Obtainable from The Retreat Association, The Central Hall, 256 Bermondsey Street, London, SE1 3UJ. **(Marks 1, 2 and 3)**

Sharing our faith

Janice Price, *Telling our Faith Story*, Church House Publishing, 1999. **(Marks 1, 2 and 6)**

James Lawrence, *Lost for Words*, CPAS*, 1999. **(Marks 1, 2 and 6)**

Both the above can be run as 'courses' to help people own and speak about their faith

John Young, *The Archbishop of York's School of Evangelism*. See York Courses*.

Finding Faith is a twenty minute audio tape designed for enquirers. Four brief stories, including the Archbishop of York. See York Courses*.

Evangelistic web site: www.rejesus.co.uk

Prayer and spirituality

Andrew Atherstone, *Search me O God: The Practice of Self-examination*, Grove Books*, 2003 (S87).

Ian Paul, *Building Your Spiritual Life*, Grove Books*, 1998 (X34).

Harold Miller, *Finding a Personal Rule of Life*, Grove Books*, 2003 (S8).

Stephen Cottrell, *Sacrament, Wholeness and Evangelism*, Grove Books*, 1999 (EV33).

John Young (ed.), *The Archbishop's School of Prayer*, with an audio tape on prayer, featuring the Archbishop of York.

Simon Stanley, *The Archbishop's School of the Sacraments*.

John Wardle, *The Archbishop's School of Healing and Wholeness*.

For the three above courses see York Courses*.

Other web sites

Unlock series of Bible studies and new ways of learning.
See www.unlock-urban.org.uk

Connect Bible studies by Scripture Union.
See www.connectbiblestudies.com

See also, Walter Wink, *Transforming Bible Studies*, Mowbray, 1990.

For details of the Anvil Trust national training programme held in regional centres, see www.workshop.org.uk or contact Tel: 0114 288816; email: office@anvil.org.uk

2. Outward-looking focus

Raymond Fung, *The Isaiah Vision*, WCC Books, 1992. Three stage process for engaging with local communities, developed out of observation of how this is happening across the globe. Can be read in an hour but may take several years to fully implement. **(Mark 2 and 6)**

Ann Morisy, *Beyond the Good Samaritan*, Continuum*, 1997. Outworking of community engagement from a more detailed and UK setting. **(Marks 2 and 6)**

Laurie Green, *Let's do Theology*, Continuum*, 2002. Applying the *see-judge-action* process, with many practical examples.

Paul Ballard and John Pritchard, *Practical Theology in Action*, SPCK, 1996. **(Marks 2 and 6)**

Samuel Wells, *Community-led Regeneration and the Local Church*, Grove Books*, 2003 (P94).

Alison White, *Getting Mission onto the Agenda of the Local Church*, Grove Books*, 1992 (EV20).

Alan Kreider, *Worship and evangelism in Pre-Christendom*, Grove Books*, 1995 (JLS32). **(Marks 1 and 2)**

John Young, *Teach Yourself Christianity*, Hodder & Stoughton, 2003.

Crucible, Crucible Subscriptions, Board for Social Responsibility, Church House, Great Smith Street, London, SW1P 3NZ. Published quarterly.

National Statistics Online: the UK's home of official statistics, reflecting Britain's economy, population and society at national and local level. Summary stories and detailed data releases are published free of charge. See www.statistics.gov.uk

Paul Wordsworth, *Living the Gospel: The Story so Far, 1999–2003*. A good summary of the process of developing MAPs (Mission Action Plans) in the York diocese. Obtainable from the Revd Paul Wordsworth, 12 Muncastergate, York, YO31 9LA. £2:00 (including p & p). Cheques/POs made out to 'YDBF'. **(Mark 2)**

See also Bob Jackson's *A Capital Idea*, a report for the London Diocese which includes analysis and observation of the role of Mission Action Plans in that diocese. Obtainable from www.london.anglican.org/CapitalIdea

Participation works: 21 techniques of community participation for the 21st century, published by the New Economics Foundation. Available from New Economics Foundation, 3 Jonathan Street, London, SE11 5NH; Tel: 020 7820 6300; email: info@neweconomics.org; www.neweconomics.org **(Marks 2 and 5)**

Marvin Weisbord and Sandra Janoff, *Future Search*, Berrett-Koehler Publishers, 1995. An action guide to finding common ground in organizations and communities. **(Marks 2 and 5)**

Geoff Shattock, *Worktalk*, a course on working well by working spiritually, published by New Wine and WorkNet, 2003. See also: www.worktalk.org.uk **(Marks 2, 4, and 5)**

Archbishop's School of Evangelism.

Archbishop's School of Christianity and Science, by John Polkinghorne.

For above two courses see York Courses*.

Transformation videos: case histories of the transformation of communities in the UK and elsewhere. Available from 'Transformations', 1 Hawthorn Villas, The Green, Wallsend-on-Tyne, NE28 7NT. See www.transformationvideo.org

Faith at work resources

Mark Greene, *Imagine: How we can reach the UK*, Authentic, 2004. The book version of the widely acclaimed essay examining the state of the nation and the state of the Church, offering a diagnosis of the blocks to mission and proposing a way forward based on disciple-making as opposed to conversion strategies. See LICC*.

Mark Greene, *Christian Life and Work*, Scripture Union, 2000. A six-part small group video resource with a leaders' guide and keyed into *Thank God It's Monday*. Suitable for use in home and work groups. See LICC*.

Mark Greene, *Thank God It's Monday*, Scripture Union, 1994. Suitable for use in home and work groups. See LICC*.

Mark Greene, *Supporting Christians at Work – without going insane*, Administry, 2001. A practical guide that explores the case for workplace ministry, unpacks the theological blocks that that have inhibited church and pastoral support in the past and provides a host of practical suggestions. See Matters Arising*.

Mark Greene, *The Three-eared Preacher*, London Bible College, 1998. A practical feedback tool developed with working pastors to help pastors improve the relevance and impact of their preaching. Only available from LICC*.

Nick Spencer, *Beyond Belief: Barriers and Bridges to Faith*, LICC*, 2003. Up-to-date qualitative research among agnostics (66% of the UK population) exploring their attitudes to church, faith and Christianity. See LICC*.

Word-for-the-Week and *Connecting with Culture*, LICC's bi-weekly emails providing short reflections from the Bible and Biblical reflection on contemporary events; email: mail@licc.org.uk

Web sites

www.faithworks.com
www.wvi.org (World Vision justice issues)

3. Seeks to find out what God wants

See under the first Mark (page 156 above) about personal spirituality and about the use of Retreats and Retreat Centres. The task is to re-work what the church is more familiar with, namely *personal* spirituality, into a pattern for developing a *corporate* spirituality and way of discerning vocation.

Roy M. Oswald and Robert E. Friedrich, Jnr, *Discerning Your Congregation's Future: A Strategic and Spiritual Approach*, Alban Institute*, 1996.

Discerning Church Vocation, Springboard resource paper distributed with *Renewing Hope for the Church* video, 2003. **(Marks 2 and 3)**

Paul Wordsworth, *Living the Gospel: The Story so Far, 1999–2003*. Report of first four years of developing Mission Action Plans in the York Diocese. Obtainable from the Revd Paul Wordsworth, 12 Muncastergate, York, YO31 9LA. £2:00 (including p & p). Cheques/POs made out to 'YDBF'. **(Marks 2 and 3)**

Other resources

Transparencies: *Pictures of Mission Through Prayer and Reflection.* Church House Publishing/CTBI, 2002. A valuable resource of varied materials for use in leading meditation. **(Marks 1, 2, and 6)**
Sue Wallace, *Multi-sensory Church*, Scripture Union. **(Marks 1 and 3)**
Sue Wallace, *Multi-sensory Prayer*, Scripture Union. **(Marks 1 and 3)**
David Spriggs, *Living Spirituality*, Administry, 2001. See Matters Arising*.
Training Event: *Catching a Vision*, provided by Matters Arising*.
Swain and Kings, *Reach Out*, SPCK, 2001. Three-term discipleship course.

Prayer resources

John Pritchard, *How to Pray*, SPCK, 2002.
Robert Warren, *An Affair of the Heart*, Highland, 1994.
Michael Mitton, *Saints at Prayer*, Kingsway, 1994.
All designed to be used by individuals and with groups.

4. Faces the cost of change and growth

Books about the future shape of church

There are many books about the Church and its future shape (see also the section on 'fresh expressions' under the fifth mark on page 164). Of particular value in helping think in fresh ways about the Church are:
Mission-shaped Church, General Synod report, Church House Publishing, 2004. **(Marks 3, 4, 5 and 6)**
Graham Tomlin, *The Provocative Church*, SPCK, 2002. **(Marks 4 and 5)**
Loren Mead, *The Once and Future Church*, Alban Institute*, 1991. **(Marks 4 and 5)**
Michael Moynagh, *Changing World, Changing Church*, Monarch Books, 2001. **(Marks 4 and 5)**
Michael Moynagh, Video: *Changing world, Changing Church*, Administry and CMS, 2001. The companion to the book, available from Matters Arising*.
John Drane, *Faith in a Changing Culture*, Marshall Pickering, 1997. **(Marks 1 and 4)**
Michael Riddell, *Threshold of the Future*, SPCK, 1997. **(Marks 4 and 6)**
James Emery White, *Rethinking the Church*, Baker Books, 1997.
James Twaites, *The Church beyond the Congregation*, Paternoster, 2002. **(Mark 4 and 5)**
Kerry Thorpe, *Doing Things Differently: Changing the Heart of the Church.* Grove Books*, 1997 (EV40). **(Marks 3 and 4)**

Books about managing change

Alban Institute*, outstanding source of creative thinking and resourcing for the whole life of the church. Web site: www.alban.org
See especially:
Gilbert Rendle, *Leading Change in the Congregation*, Alban Institute*, 1998. **(Mark 4)**
Loren Mead, *Transforming Congregations for the Future*, Alban Institute*, 1994. **(Mark 4)**
Roy M. Oswald, *Power Analysis of a Congregation*, revised and updated edition, Alban Institute*, 1998. **(Mark 4 and all the others)**
David Cormack, *Change Directions: New Ways Forward for Your Life, Church and Business*, Monarch, 1995. Starts from the personal and leads into the corporate, thus linking spiritual motivation with change. **(Marks 1 and 4)**
Robert Warren, *Launching a Missionary Congregation*, CPAS*, 1995. Five session study guide with interesting group work activities to help people think of church in new ways.

Conflict management

Bridge Builders is a programme of the London Mennonite Centre (LMC). It provides training, mediation, consultancy, and related services for all Christian churches and denominations in Britain. Contact: The Director of Bridge Builders, London Mennonite Centre, 14 Shepherds Hill, London, N6 5AQ; www.menno.org.uk
Charles Raven, *Conflict and Growth*, Grove Books*, 1998 (S64).
Speed B. Leas, *Moving Your Church Through Conflict*, Alban Institute*, 1985.
Teal Trust: see www.teal.org.uk
Training Event: *Managing change – avoiding conflict*, provided by Matters Arising*.

5. *Operates as a community*

Leadership books

Among the many books on leadership some of particular value are:
Henri Nouwen, *In the Name of Jesus*, Darton, Longman & Todd, 1989. Reflections on the temptations of Christ and what they have to say about a leadership style reflective of Christ. **(Mark 5)**
Thomas R. Hawkins, *The Learning Congregation*, Westminster John Knox Press, 1997. A helpful book on changing role of leaders in a post-modern and participative culture. **(Mark 5)**
Jonathan Gledhill, *Leading a Local Church*, SPCK, 2003. **(Mark 5)**
J. Nelson, *Leading, Managing, Ministering*, Canterbury Press, 1998. **(Mark 5)**
Stephen Covey, *The Seven Habits of Highly Effective People*, Simon & Schuster, 1989. **(Mark 5)**
Chris Edmonson, *Fit to Lead*, Darton, Longman & Todd, 2002. **(Mark 5)**

Steven Croft, *Ministry in Three Dimensions*, Darton, Longman & Todd, 1999. **(Mark 5)**

James Lawrence, *Growing Leaders*, CPAS*, 2004. **(Mark 5)**

Chris Edmondson, *Minister: Love Thyself! Sustaining Healthy Ministry*, Grove Books*, 2000 (P83). **(Mark 5)**

James Lawrence, *Growing Leaders: Reflections on Leadership, Life and Jesus*, CPAS*, 2004.

Leadership resources

MODEM is a 'national and ecumenical network formed as a charity to encourage better understanding between leadership, management and ministry.' Details from: Modem, CTBI, Inter-Church House, 35–41 Lower Marsh, London, SE1 7RI; www.modem.uk.com

The Teal Trust: Helping leaders be leaders in the church, in society and in the workplace. See their web site: www.teal.org.uk

There is much good material from the Directory of Social Change, such as M. Hudson, *Managing without Profit*, 2002. **(Marks 4, 5 and 6)**

Leadership courses

Clergy Leadership Programme, from the Leadership Institute: Excellent material that integrates theology with best current management and leadership practice. Offers a range of national residential courses in Canterbury and Durham for bishops, deans, archdeacons and parochial clergy, as well as supporting diocesan programmes. Highly recommended. Executive Director, the Revd Rob Mackintosh. CD-based resources for individual or group learning. Contact Jean Evans. Tel: 01366 382969; email: tlioffice@aol.com. See www.tli.org.uk **(Mark 5)**

The Arrow Course: For leaders (ordained and lay) aged 25–40 concerned for mission and prepared to change. An integrated learning process focusing on call, character and competency in leadership. Carefully designed to help significant change take place in participants' lives. Web site: www.cpas.org.uk/leadership/arrow; email: arrow@cpas.org.uk; Tel: 01926 458419. Currently headed up by the Revd James Lawrence. **(Mark 5)**

Community building

Michael Schluter and David Lee, *The R Factor*, Hodder & Stoughton, 1993. **(Mark 5)**

Work produced by The Relationship Foundation originally to help organizations and businesses to build better relationships.

Building a Relational Church is a programme designed by the Jubilee Centre to help you look at relationship-building in the life of your church. The audit includes a questionnaire designed to assess whether the right environment for building relationships with a congregation is being created. The audit pack can be downloaded from the Jubilee Centre web site: www.jubilee-centre.org or http://jubilee.iedesign.co.uk

Pamela Evans, *Building the Body*, BRF, 2002. **(Mark 5)**

Jean Vanier, *From Brokenness to Community*, Paulist Press, 1992.

Lay ministry and ministry teams

Stewart C. Zabriskie, *Total Ministry: Reclaiming the Ministry of All God's People*, Alban Institute*, 1995. **(Mark 5)**
Robin Greenwood, *Transforming Church: Liberation Structures for Ministry*, SPCK, 2002. **(Mark 5)**
Andrew Daweswell, *Ministry Leadership Teams: Theory and Practice in Effective Collaborative Ministry*, Grove Books*, 2003 (P93). **(Mark 5)**
Chris Skilton, *Leadership Teams: Clergy and Lay Leadership in the Local Church*, Grove Books*, 1999 (P78). **(Mark 5)**
David Mayer, *Our Gifts: Identifying and Developing Leaders*, Willow Creek; www.willowcreek.org.uk

Fresh expressions of church, including Cell Church

Leonardo Boff, *Ecclesiogenesis: The Base Communities Reinvent the Church*, Orbis, 1986. **(Marks 1, 4, 5 and 6)**
James O'Halloran, *Signs of Hope: Developing Small Christian Communities*, Orbis, 1991. **(Marks 1, 4, 5 and 6)**
Steven Croft, *Transforming Communities*, Darton, Longman & Todd, 2002. **(Mark 5)**
Stuart Murray and Anne Wilkinson-Hayes, *Hope From The Margins: New Ways of Being Church*, Grove Books*, 2000 (EV49). **(Mark 5)**
Phil Potter, *The Challenge of Cell Church*, CPAS*/BRF, 2001. **(Mark 5)**
Tony Hardy, *Cell Church Values*, CPAS*. Ready-to-use materials offering a thorough grounding in cell-church basics.
Anglican Church Planting Initiative led by Bob and Mary Hopkins. See www.acpi.org.uk, also: www.cellchurch.co.uk or www.accn.org.uk
George Lings, *Encounters on the Edge*, a series of quarterly investigations into new ways of being church. For details see: www.encountersontheedge.org.uk
David Beer, *Fifty Ways to Help your Church Grow*, Kingsway, 2000. **(Marks 5 and 6)**
Jeffrey John, *Going for Growth*, Affirming Catholicism. See www.affirmingcatholicism.org.uk **(Marks 1, 5, 6 and 7)**
A Church Without Walls, The Church of Scotland, 2001. See www.churchwithoutwalls.org.uk **(Marks 2 to 6)**

Training for Cell and Small Group Work and Church Planting

www.resourcechurchplanting.co.uk
www.tribalgeneration.com
www.emergingchurch.infro

6. Makes room for all

See under the first Mark and process evangelism courses.
For research on the spirituality of people who do not go to church see the paper entitled '*Spirituality of the Unchurched*' by David Hay of

Nottingham University. It can be downloaded from
www.martynmission.cam.ac.uk/BIAMSHay.htm
Philip Richter and Leslie Francis, *Gone But Not Forgotten*, Darton, Longman
& Todd, 1998. Thorough and instructive research into reasons why people
drift away from church, with many insights as to how to make room for
those not inclined to stay around. **(Marks 5 and 6)**
A. Jamieson, *A Churchless Faith*, SPCK, 2002. Interesting research (mainly
from New Zealand but applicable to UK) about people who have stopped
going to church but have kept the faith. Main reason cited is that established
churches stifle individual spiritual growth. **(Marks 1 and 6)**
See also Bob Jackson's *A Capital Idea*, a report for the London diocese that
includes evidence that much of the growth of the church in that diocese is
coming from churches learning to be multicultural. Obtainable from
www.london.anglican.org/CapitalIdea
James Lawrence, *Lost for Words*, CPAS*, 1999. Available both as a
paperback book and also as three courses: one for children, one for young
people and one for young adults. **(Marks 1, 2 and 6)**
Paul Mogford, *Fifty Easy Outreach Ideas*, Kingsway, 2000. **(Marks 2 and 6)**
John Hattam, *Families Finding Faith*, CPAS*, 2000. **(Marks 2 and 6)**
Pearse and Matthews, *We must stop meeting like this*, Kingsway, 1999.
(Mark 6)
Key, Smith, Richardson and Dorey, *Booked out*, CPAS*, 1995. **(Mark 6)**
John Holmes, *Vulnerable Evangelism*, Grove Books*, 2001 (EV54). **(Marks
1 and 6)**
Jackie Cray, *Being family friendly*, Administry, 2001. See Matters Arising*.
Graham Cray and Paul Simmonds, *Being Culturally Relevant*, Administry,
2000. See Matters Arising*.
Training event: *Being a More User-friendly Church*, provided by Matters
Arising*.

Children and youth

Organizations
The following organizations all offer resources, training and advice. Contact
them for further details.
BRF (Bible Reading Fellowship), 'Barnabas' is the children's section of BRF.
In addition to training and resources, 'Barnabas Live' events bring the Bible
alive for children. Tel: 01865 319700; email: info@brf.org.uk;
web site: www.brf.org.uk
CPAS* (Church Pastoral Aid Society), major Anglican evangelistic
organization. Activities include camps for children and teenagers.
Tel: 01926 334242; email: mail@cpas.org.uk; web site: www.cpas.org.uk
CURBS (Children in Urban Situations), for those working with children in
urban situations. Tel: 01737 642522; email: info@curbsproject.org.uk;
web site: www.curbsproject.org.uk
Rural Sunrise, part of Sunrise Ministries, which works with small and
rural churches. Tel: 01323 832083; email: ruralmissions@zetnet.co.uk;
web site: www.ruralmissions.org.uk/sunrise.htm

Scripture Union, a major non-denominational evangelistic organization.
Tel: 01908 856000; email: info@scriptureunion.org.uk; web site:
www.scriptureunion.org.uk

Books

Monica Cook, *Children's Work Audit*, available from Rural Sunrise.
See www.ruralmissions.org.uk/sunrise.htm
Graham Cray, *Youth Congregations and the Emerging Church*, Grove
Books*, 2002 (EV57).
Philip Clark and Geoff Pearson, *Kidz Klubs: The Alpha of Children's
Evangelism?* Grove Books*, 2001 (EV45).
Margaret Withers, *Fired up . . . not burnt out*, BRF, 2001 (a training course
for children's leaders).
The *Growing in Faith* series for children's evangelism, CPAS*/Scripture
Union, including:

- Francis Bridger, *Children Finding Faith*. Bridger's combination of
  child-development sensitivity with theological insight provides
  an excellent introduction to faith-sharing with children. £6.99;
- Penny Frank, *Bringing Children to Faith*. A workbook to help
  church teams implement good practice for children's evangelism.
  £7.00;
- David Bell and Rachel Heathfield, *Mission Possible*. A 64-page
  resource book to help plan holiday clubs, family events, schools'
  work, church services.£7.00.

Penny Frank, *Every Child a Chance to Choose: The challenge of children's
evangelism*, CPAS*/Kingsway. Penny Frank takes a critical look at current
practice and proposes practical steps for reaching today's children.
James Lawrence, *Lost for Words*, CPAS*, 1999. Available both as a
paperback book and also as three courses: one for children, one for
young people and one for young adults. **(Marks 1, 2 and 6)**
Stephen Cottrell *et al*, *Youth Emmaus*, Church House Publishing, 2003.
Aimed at young people aged 11–16. A youth version of the *Emmaus
Nurture* course. **(Marks 1 and 6)**
Bob Jackson, *A Capital Idea*, analysis of the causes of growth in the
London Diocese with insights that cover many marks, not least that of
making room for all. Obtainable from www.london.anglican.org/CapitalIdea
(Mark 6)
Viz-A-Viz has a team of 40 people working in evangelism, schools work,
training and media production. See www.vizaviz.org
Youthwork: www.youthwork.co.uk is a joint site hosted by Youthwork
Magazine, Oasis, The Salvation Army, Youth For Christ and Spring Harvest.
Their aim is to work together to equip and resource the Church for effective
youth work and ministry.

7. Does a few things and does them well

Doing less/Prioritizing

'Do you want to bear fruit for God? Simplify your life. Do fewer things and do them better'. From a fine sermon by Austin Farrar, entitled *Pruning for Perfection*, in Austin Farrar, *The End of Man*, Hodder & Stoughton, 1975 (p. 175)

Stephen Covey, *The Seven Habits of Highly Effective People*, Simon & Schuster, 1989.

Pamela Evans, *Driven Beyond the Call of God*, BRF, 1999.

James Lawrence, *Growing Leaders*, CPAS*/BRF, 2004.

Tom and Christine Sine, *Living on Purpose*, Monarch, 2002.

Os Guinness, *The Call*, Authentic Lifestyle, 2001.

Gordon MacDonald, *Ordering your Private World*, Highland, 2003.

Patrick Klingaman, *Finding Rest When the Work is Never Done*, Chariot Victor Publishing, 2000.

Ajith Fernando, *Jesus Driven Ministry*, IVP, 2003.

Rick Warren, *The Purpose Driven Life*, Zondervan, 2003.

John Adair, *How to Find your Vocation*, Canterbury Press, 2002.

Henri Nouwen, *In the Name of Jesus*, Darton, Longman & Todd, 1989.

Doing things well

Patsy Kettle, *Coping with Stress at Church*, Administry, 1998. Available from Matters Arising*.

Training event: *Managing Time, Paper, and People*, provided by Matters Arising*.

Aubrey Malphurs, *Advanced Strategic Planning: A New Model for Church and Ministry Leaders*, Baker Book House Company, 1999. From Matters Arising*.

Larry Bossidy and Ram Charan, *Execution: The Discipline of Getting Things Done*, Random House, 2002.

Bill Hybels, *Courageous Leadership*, Zondervan, 2002, Chapters 2 and 3.

Walter Wright, *Relational Leadership*, Paternoster, 2000, Chapter 3.

Thomas J. Peters and Robert H. Waterman, *In Search of Excellence*, Harper & Row, 1982.

Occasional offices

Wesley Carr, *Brief Encounters*, SPCK, 1985.

The work of facilitation

Two major works

George Lovell, *Consultancy, Ministry and Mission: A Handbook for Practicioners and Work Consultants in Christian Organizations*, Burns & Oates, 2000. The fruit of his work as Director of Avec from 1976–91 and his work as a Methodist minister and freelance Consultant. **(The whole process)**

Anne Hope and Sally Timmel, *Training for Transformation: A Handbook For Community Workers*, Intermediate Technologies Publications, 1984. In three volumes. Provides a wealth of practical help from a two-thirds world perspective, developing Paulo Friere's work and insights. The aim is to 'assist workers in the field who are encouraging the development of self-reliant creative communities'. **(The whole process)**

Consultants and Facilitators

From within church structures

In the Church of England there are a number of people within diocesan structures who often work as consultants and facilitators. They are normally sector ministers such as parish development officers, missioners, adult/lay training officers, etc. Archdeacons can usually help by pointing people in the right direction for such people.

Other denominations have similar sector ministers.

From beyond church structures

Just three examples of such sources are:

CPAS* (Church Pastoral Aid Society). As well as providing published resources on leadership and evangelism with a focus on the all-age church, CPAS provides a wide variety of training and consultancy for church leaders. A good first point of contact is the CPAS Ministry Consultant in your area.

Matters Arising* (formerly 'Administry') has a consultancy service which is a 'tailor-made' facilitation and advice service. It ranges from a one day review of activities and structures through to a year long relationship, coaching and mentoring a leadership team.

CMS (Church Mission Society) seeks to be a movement of people in mission. CMS is able to offer consultations to help individuals and churches picture a church that is globally connected and locally committed. CMS also offers advice on Missional Leadership and Missional groups as well as a variety of cross-cultural experiences.

Contact details: CMS Partnership House, 157 Waterloo Road, London, SE1 8UU; Tel: 020 7928 8681; web site: www.cms-uk.org